FINANCIAL SUCCESS:

TEN SHORTCUTS TO
A PROFITABLE BUSINESS

JERRY PRADIER, AInstIB

Order this book online at www.trafford.com
or email orders@trafford.com

Most Trafford titles are also available at major online book retailers.

Note for Librarians: A cataloguing record for this book is available from Library
and Archives Canada at www.collectionscanada.ca/amicus/index-e.html

Printed in Victoria, BC, Canada.

ISBN: 978-1-4251-6149-1 (soft)
ISBN: 978-1-4251-7747-8 (ebook)

*We at Trafford believe that it is the responsibility of us all, as both individuals
and corporations, to make choices that are environmentally and socially sound.
You, in turn, are supporting this responsible conduct each time you purchase a
Trafford book, or make use of our publishing services. To find out how you are
helping, please visit www.trafford.com/responsiblepublishing.html*

*Our mission is to efficiently provide the world's finest, most comprehensive
book publishing service, enabling every author to experience success.
To find out how to publish your book, your way, and have it available
worldwide, visit us online at www.trafford.com*

Trafford rev. 6/25/2009

 www.trafford.com

North America & international
toll-free: 1 888 232 4444 (USA & Canada)
phone: 250 383 6864 ♦ fax: 250 383 6804 ♦ email: info@trafford.com

To my parents who are with me daily. To Mary A. Pradier, Tony Pradier, Angel Cole, Zoë and Kathleen Moore who are with me from afar.

CONTENTS

ACKNOWLEDGEMENTS

THIS is my thanks to the many individuals who have contributed to my education, both emotional and intellectual, that enabled me to produce the ideas in this book. I also thank the many clients, colleagues and friends who have given me the support that has helped me complete this task.

To my friends; Marc Powell, Tom Clark, Tom Fleming, Cyndi Peters, Sherri Pochop, Barb Filippone, Clayton Collier, Holly Woods and Carol Annand, who support and challenge me to be better than I am.

To my associates who have contributed materially to the successful completion of this project; Willard Barth and Jim Black for their unique perspectives and inputs as authors and business executives, Todd Patrick (www.toddpatrickphotography.com) for photographic support, and Kirsten Michel of 8.31 Productions, LLC, for her thorough and precise editing.

To my friends and support system Bridget Mactavish, Lauren McDonell and Tari Williams who are always here to help me clarify my ideas as students and teachers.

To the many clients who have given me a laboratory to perfect my skills and prove that these concepts work as advertised.

Finally, to my readers who support my work and professional goals.

Thanks to all of you.

FOREWORD

WHEN Jerry first asked me if I would write a foreword for his new book, I was honored. When I read it, I was THRILLED! In my career as a professional speaker and peak performance coach, I have made studying success my top priority. I have read hundreds of books, attended seminars all over the country, immersed myself in home study courses and mentored with some of the most amazing teachers of our time. Experience has shown that the best teachers are the ones who can take what seems complex, and break it down into actionable, practical steps.

In this book Jerry has taken his experience as a businessman and executive coach and presents the reader with a very specific plan on how to create a successful business. One of the things I have always admired about Jerry is his ability to "cut through the BS" and give you valuable insight into what you are doing right, what you are doing wrong, and what you can do more effectively to achieve your goals. He doesn't pull punches, and at the same time, you know that he is coming from a very deep place of wanting the very best for you.

I believe that Jerry has succeeded in bringing this same character strength across in this wonderful book. His direct approach has allowed him to fill this book with immense value. Every page is filled with principles that will allow you to create a business that not only rewards you, but also creates an empowering environment for your employees, and your community.

Jerry is one of the unique individuals who understands that creating a successful business, of any kind, is an "inside job". Not only does he share with you step-by-step processes on the most vital aspects of running your business, he also shares the psychology behind it.

One of the trainings that I get asked to do most is based on "Modeling" the success of others. In this training, I discuss how there are three very specific areas that you need to be aware of when attempting to model another person's success. Most people are only aware of one. If you ask someone what they need to focus on when studying someone who is getting great results, they will usually say, "You need to say what they say, and do what they do." Yet, how many people do you know, who say the same things, and do the same things that a top producer is saying and doing, yet they don't come close to getting the same results? The challenge is that these people are applying the "strategies" that the top producer uses, but are missing the two most important ingredients, the psychological and emotional factors that fuel the "strategies."

Jerry does a phenomenal job of not only teaching the step-by-step strategies of how to build a successful business, but also address the "reason" and "motive" for doing these things. It is my belief that these are the core differences between success, or failure for any venture.

It is rare that a book comes along that covers so much so clearly. I wish that this had been available to me earlier in my career. It is a "handbook" for building a successful business, and a successful life.

Willard Barth, Peak Performance Coach
Willard Barth Enterprises, willardbarth.com

INTRODUCTION

"Life is short. Art is long. Occasion is sudden and dangerous.
Experience is deceitful. And Judgment is difficult."
- HIPPOCRATES, GREEK PHYSICIAN

WHAT entrepreneur decides to start a business without the hope and expectation of unimaginable success? "Success," to those I counsel, is translated in many ways. Some view success as being independent. To others, success is having more time for themselves and their families—not having to report to others. Still, others believe that business success is achieving the ability to "give back" or simply to "give" to others. Some even view success in terms of creating a business that will be bought by a larger company, leaving them with the freedom and money to move on to start another challenging enterprise.

However, the underlying goal, no matter what reason you give for starting your business, should be to create a profitable business. None of these stated goals or desires would be possible if the business was losing money or barely hanging on. If the business is not profitable, the owner would not have the resources or energy to accomplish any of her other stated goals.

This observation is least apparent, I believe, to those who want to create a business for some altruistic purpose. These prospective owners tend to think of making money and financial success as somewhat selfish, unclean, and beneath them. For example, I work with many kind hearts (well-meaning philanthropists) who have lofty goals of feeding the poor or providing medical care to invalids. Their stated goals are admirable but they are unrealistic when they say they do not care about making money or that they couldn't care less about becoming successful businesspersons.

My first question to them is, "Why would you want to go into business if you already have all the resources you need to achieve your goals?" If they admit that they don't have these resources, my follow-up question is, "How do you expect to get the resources when your business is failing or when the resources you have are being eaten up with little to no return from the business you are creating?"

Running a business is difficult enough when you create a business for the right reasons and with the right attitude. Starting a business based on the wrong motivation dooms the business to stagnation and failure at the outset.

In my opinion, if you go into business, a major goal for you should be to make it profitable because that is the **primary** measure of success. However, even if entrepreneurs accept this principle and enter business for the right reasons and with the right motivation, many fail because they tend to do the wrong things, following the lead of many others who are in business doing things the hard way. It is the classic case of the blind leading the blind.

This book emerges out of over 25 years of owning or running independent, private and public businesses. These suggestions apply to not-for-profit and for-profit businesses alike. It is intended to help you benefit from this extensive experience and find ways to keep management the fun activity you anticipated when it was just your dream.

The purpose of this book is not to give lengthy descriptions of how to implement the shortcuts. Instead, it offers a clear description of the shortcuts so that the reader will be able to identify when to implement them and leaves it to the manager to apply the art of management in judging how to implement them. In many cases, however, we will point you to resources where you can find extensive information on how to implement the strategies.

The purpose of this book is to incite the creative juices to flow. From here, you will be able to determine when and why to apply the shortcuts. There are plenty of other sources to help you explore how to apply them.

Two sources this book points to are www.AskJerry-TheFixer.com and www.OnlineBusinessKnowledge.com. These sites are sources of information and management tools you may access to upgrade your entrepreneurial skills. As indicated on the book's cover, there are more than $250 worth of copyrighted management tools and examples that you may use as a purchaser of this volume.

You may read this book from beginning to end but it is not necessary to do so. You can get a lot of benefit by reading the chapters out of sequence in order to take advantage of specific shortcuts.

Here's wishing you all the best for a successful and profitable entrepreneurial experience.

"Every accomplishment starts with the decision to try."
—ANONYMOUS

"Never has 'No' or 'Can't' resulted in a success."
—JERRY "THE FIXER" PRADIER, BUSINESS OPTIMIZATION EXPERT

1.

CREATE WINNING HABITS

"Motivation is what gets you started. Habit is what keeps you going."

- JIM ROHN, BUSINESS AND SPORTS COACH

W E cannot avoid the subject of character development and personal habits when we talk about growing a successful business quickly. There are two reasons for this. The first reason why the development of certain character traits is so important is because the identity of the independent or private business and the identity of the owner are virtually indistinguishable. As the owner of a business, whatever people think of you, they will think of your business and whatever they think of your business, they identify with you. There's no escaping this phenomenon, especially in the case of emerging businesses. This is why startup businesses that are seeking bank financing need to provide the personal tax statements of the owners as evidence of financial stability and trustworthiness. By extension, your business will be identified with your employees. So, it is necessary that the employees accept and practice the values of the business and owner.

The second reason why we need to talk about character is related to the first. People do not want to do business with people they don't like or trust. So, it is to your benefit to be the type of person whom people like and trust. This is where your character comes into play. Your character is revealed in your deliberate, habitual actions. Deliberate, habitual actions are synonymous with character traits. Reflex actions, such as recoiling when you feel a sharp pain, are not products of deliberation (thought) or habit. Reflex actions are the uncontrollable responses to pain or other physical stimuli. Deliberate actions arise out of conscious or subconscious decisions and repeating deliberate actions develops habits.

This chapter talks about character traits that are most visible to consumers when they make the conscious or subconscious decision about whether they want to do business with you. You, the owner, want every potential client to choose to do business with you. So you want your business to reflect only the best traits you instill in the business through your personality.

How do we demonstrate these character traits? Well, the easiest way is to habitually act in ways that demonstrate these traits. The ancient Greek philosopher, Aristotle, understood this phenomenon. He said that you can tell the character of a person by observing how the person acts. Your actions, over time, display your character. Doing the same things repeatedly until they become part of our nature develops character traits within us.

In *Entrepreneurship 101*, we are encouraged to identify three crucial concepts to help define our businesses and to help guide the business through its growth and development phases. These concepts are Mission, Vision and Values. The **mission** is the purpose of the business, the statement of work that the business is dedicated to performing. The **vision** is a view of the business in its most perfect or successful state, having overcome all obstacles and limitations that threaten its success. The **values** are those positive characteristics by which you want the public to identify the business. They are the characteristics that make the business attractive to potential clients.

It is important to develop, for our businesses and within ourselves, those character traits by which we want our businesses and ourselves to be identified. The aim of this chapter is to present the most visible characteristics we should work to create. They are the most visible because they are the traits that determine how we interact with the customers. Potential clients will most easily observe these traits in our daily operations.

Some of these traits or habits will seem counterintuitive but the most successful sales people will tell you that their success is based on adopting and displaying these traits. So, here they are: Patience, Persistence, Helpfulness, Generosity, Caring, and Honesty.

Patience

Impatience, on the part of business owners, can doom businesses to premature failure or chronic struggling to succeed. When an owner lacks patience, he will start to show the symptoms of irritability, edginess, and annoyance. He will react to his environment rather than act on his environment. The difference is that when one reacts, one is being controlled by something external. When one acts, one is in control and is following a predetermined course of action.

Owners need to guard against displaying impatience at all stages of business development. Recognizing when impatience occurs, can be a big help in preventing this irrational reaction to stressful circumstances. One sign that an entrepreneur is not practicing patience is when she has committed to start a business and realizes she is not fully prepared.

I met with a couple that was starting a franchise a few years ago who asked for help in starting their new business. When I asked about their timeline, I learned that they had committed to sign the agreements the following week. Upon further questioning, I learned that they had not selected an attorney or accountant, had not signed a partnership agreement and had given their notices to current employers that they were leaving their jobs. Clearly, they had not adequately prepared or asked the right questions about this franchise opportunity. We had to scramble to correct some of these oversights but, luckily, they were able to get an extension from the franchiser. Even with the extension, we didn't have enough time to correct every problem. So, the business struggled for several months after startup.

Many entrepreneurs don't devote the necessary amount of time to adequately prepare to start the business. This is sometimes due to their overly enthusiastic expectations of success. At other times, this is due to failing to work through the preparatory steps that are crucial to starting the business properly. In other words, they do not create a business plan prior to making the commitment. This situation is the result of impatience.

For older, struggling businesses, impatience causes the owners to panic and scramble to turn their problems around immediately—an impossibility given the growth of systems that have caused the problems to develop. I try to remind owners in this situation that the problem wasn't created overnight, so the solution must take a while to take effect. It stands to reason that if problems have developed over months or years, they cannot be corrected overnight. Often, the owner's panic is understandable because the situation is usually at the point of total disaster. However, impatience can only force the owner to make rash decisions to correct a quickly deteriorating situation. Lack of patience causes one to react reflexively rather than according to a rational plan.

Patience, on the other hand, helps us realize that running a business correctly depends on a developmental process. A business is like a human in many ways. It goes through stages of birth and growth that cannot be artificially altered. Just as a child cannot immediately go from learning to turn over in the crib to walking without learning to sit up then crawl, a business cannot go from conception to immediate success without working through a marketing strategy and growing a clientele. If the marketing strategy is not planned well or if there is none, the business will have development problems. If your method of growing a clientele is haphazard, the business will lack the sustenance it needs to grow.

As a business owner, if you don't recognize that a situation, which took months or years to develop, cannot be undone or turned around in a day, you are bound to make the wrong decisions or give up completely out of frustration. It doesn't matter what time limit you're under to fix the problem, you have no chance of turning around a struggling business immediately. You have to use a creative way to gain more time, if you're faced with a hard deadline, and revert to your original plan to fix the problem within the time you have. I have never seen a case where impatiently making rash decisions to fix a bad situation did not result in destroying the business or in fueling the problem longer than necessary.

One of the most important traits you need to develop is patience. You should practice patience by taking sufficient time to adequately prepare a business plan. The plan, in turn, will nourish your patience if you use it to run the business. It will give you the heads up you need to adjust to the unexpected negative and positive outcomes you will undoubtedly encounter. And in return, you will be less pressured to act impulsively in reaction to negative forces in the business environment.

Persistence

Persistence refers to the practice of not giving up when you encounter problems and obstacles to your progress. It does not refer to stubbornness. Persistence is empowering. Stubbornness is destructive.

Persistence is acting based on an analysis of the obstacle,

defining its parameters and limitations, and finding a way to circumvent or neutralize the power that the obstacle represents. Stubbornness is represented by forcefully plowing into the obstacle and trying to overcome it with force (emotional outbursts, money, physical effort) alone. This is not to say that force has no role in overcoming business obstacles but, blind, brute force is normally ineffective.

Persistence requires the application of courageous, perceptive, focused, and timed force that meets the needs of the situation. Let's examine each of these elements.

Persistence is based on courage. When faced with a problem that needs to be overcome, our first instinct is to exhibit fear or to quit. This problem, however, is an opportunity to practice courage because courage cannot be possible without fear of a danger and without having the option to give up or run away. When we decide to act in spite of fear and to fight instead of run, we are being courageous.

But courage, alone is not persistence because courage alone is foolhardiness. Courage has to be controlled by a complete understanding of the situation one is encountering. This means that we must analyze the problem in terms of the risk, imminence, and power it has. By knowing what we are facing, we can determine the best way to overcome or manage it.

This brings us to the third element of persistence, focus. We must make a decision whether it is best to destroy the obstacle, work around it, ignore it (because the risk is slight or the effects are weak), or manage it in a way to limit its effect. The best course of action, in almost all cases, is to apply only enough force that is necessary to overcome the problem. Otherwise, you will be wasting resources. You would not drive a nail into wood using a cannon; you would use a nail gun. By contrast, you would not try to stop a charging elephant with a flyswatter; you would use an elephant rifle. The same goes for business problems. Match the correction to the problem. Don't fire your staff if you learn of internal theft, you would find out who is doing the stealing and deal with each one appropriately and that correction might range from administrative action, to punishment or dismissal.

Finally, the timing of the correction is just as important as the other elements. It is usually best to make corrections as soon as the problem is found to prevent the problem from getting worse and harder to correct. Sometimes you may have to wait to apply the correction because you don't know enough about the nature of the problem and want to prevent applying an inappropriate correction. You must also determine a time limit for applying your correction to avoid the problem of stubbornly applying an ineffective correction. Usually, if a correction does not take effect within a certain amount of time, it is appropriate for you to try something else.

By following these guidelines, you can assure yourself that you are managing your business rather than letting your business control you. When you're managing your business, you are saving time and money by taking actions that help grow your profits.

Helpfulness

This characteristic is directly related to the reason you might have gone into business. Do you want to own a business to simply make money or to make money while helping others get what they desire or need? Which reason is more desirable? Which one speaks to the higher purpose in life? I'm sure you will agree that the second reason is not solely self-centered or selfish. The second is altruistic as well as self-interested. In business, it is important to have both goals. Being totally focused outwardly is as bad as being totally focused inwardly (Selfishness). There has to be a balance of both.

Wanting to help others changes the way one acts during the sales process. If you simply want to make a sale, you might be tempted to do anything at all to get someone to buy. If you want to make a sale that will truly help the client, making the sale *at all costs* will be less important to you. This attitude of helpfulness will be obvious in your body language and words. If making the sale at any cost is your goal, your need to sell will affect your approach, your facial expressions, your choice of words and your reflex responses. Your potential customers will be able to read your motivation long before you realize what you're communicating to them.

In sales classes I teach, I encounter the false assumption that the sales process is, by nature, totally selfish. This is the first attitude I have to change before I am able to teach effective sales techniques. For too many years, the image of the huckster has dominated our view of salespeople. This is not an accurate representation of the sales process, which, ideally, is a win-win encounter for the customer and the salesperson.

For this reason, I encourage those new sales people I coach to walk into a sales situation with no desire to sell anything. They soon learn that they sell more by not trying to sell. What I encourage them to substitute for the desire to make a sale is the desire to help. A successful sales person will try to find out what the buyer wants and needs, and then try to provide the best solution to meet the buyer's needs. If you do not have the best solution and you point the buyer to the best solution, you have just created a relationship of trust. Chances are, it will be much easier for you to sell to that buyer in the future.

The importance of relationship building cannot be stressed too much in marketing. Suzanne Richardson of *Early To Rise* states:

> There should be no difference between what you
> think of as "marketing" and what you think of as "re-
> lationship building." Essentially, they are one and the

same. Good marketing - no matter where or how you're doing it - is about building a relationship. Every time you speak to a customer, every time you write an article, every time you post a comment on a blog, every time you answer a question on a forum - it's all marketing, because it all reflects back on your business and its ability to fulfill your customers' needs.

Helpfulness is one of those foundations of a trusting relationship. It encompasses the following traits that are necessary to develop relationships that grow clientele.

Generosity

Closely related to helpfulness is the characteristic of generosity. You might ask, "What does generosity have to do with selling?" "Isn't it the opposite of selling?" "Doesn't generosity refer to giving?" For the answers to these questions, refer to the discussion on *helpfulness*. Certainly, these concepts are counterintuitive but, because they are counterintuitive, they are powerful sales tools.

Many of our assumptions about how to make sales, though false, are widely held because we associate selling with the apparent con artists that we see on late night TV. In fact, selling has more to do with giving than getting. We should want to give a solution to a problem or give the client what she really needs or wants. Our own needs should not be the priority. Our priority should be to help the client.

The more clearly the client senses that we want to help her, the more sales we will make. As an executive coach, I stress this principle to each sales executive who is my protégé. Those that become successful faster are the ones who forget to sell.

With this attitude, you are relieved of the pressure that comes with convincing the buyer to purchase what you're selling. Relieved of this pressure, you are more likely to focus on developing the relationship of trust that must be the foundation of every buying decision. Without this pressure, you will be more willing to spend the time necessary to listen to the buyer to find out his needs and wants. You will no longer be focusing on your needs but, on the buyer's needs. Giving your time and attention is the most personal and effective display of generosity.

Honesty

Treating everyone you deal with honestly is an absolute necessity in building a thriving and carefree business. Since marketing is your primary purpose, every ad, every promotion, every claim you make must be unquestionable in the minds of your listeners. The essence of honesty is truthfulness in word and action. The absence of this characteristic makes everything we say suspect. If nothing we say can be relied on to be truthful, how can we have an effective advertising campaign? Would any guarantee mean anything? Obviously, we would have problems attracting clients and customers if we were not totally honest with the public.

No one wants to do business with anyone he can't trust. No one in his right mind would even want to be associated with you on a social level. How much will your reputation for honesty affect your business? No one can say with certainty but would you want to risk the loss to find out?

Honesty is a component of helpfulness because it is always directed toward others. Some might want to debate this claim but the reason lie detectors work so well is based on this principle. It is much easier to lie to others than it is to lie to yourself.

While you can find examples of dishonesty that have endured for several years, almost all of these examples come from larger businesses where the owners and managers are able to hide behind the complexity of the organizations. Hiding is much more difficult where you are identified as your company and you are in the forefront, dealing directly with the public. Is this a risk you want your company—your dream—to take?

Caring

Closely related to the first characteristic is that of caring. Caring, in this context, is feeling and exhibiting concern and empathy for others. It is also the concern, empathy, and consideration for the needs and values of others. Caring is the attitude that leads to the actions of generosity and honesty. Caring is the desire to satisfy the needs of others for their benefit as well as for yours. Caring is the opposite characteristic of the ruthlessness displayed by Gordon Gekko in the 1987 movie, *Wall Street*. You might recall that, Gekko, played by Michael Douglas, espoused greed—looking out for Number One. He says,

"It's all about bucks, kid.

The rest is conversation."

Nothing mattered beyond what he could get for himself.

This attitude is so transparent that if you display it to potential customers, they would not want to do business with you. They will sense that when it comes to a choice between you and them, your choice will always be for your benefit. Few would want to do business with someone who would do anything for the fast buck. Buyers are concerned with their own desires and needs. The opposite of caring is selfishness. This is the epitome of a win-lose relationship.

Key Points

1. The market does not make a distinction between the small, independent business and its owner and employees.
2. Your personality and character are imprinted on your business in the mind of the public.

3. You can gain an advantage in the marketplace by adopting certain desirable personal characteristics that the market sees as beneficial to its goals, needs and desires.
4. The most helpful personal characteristics for achieving business success are patience, persistence, helpfulness, generosity, honesty and caring.
5. By adopting these characteristics, you will give your business' potential for success a boost.

"You cannot climb the ladder of success dressed in the costume of failure."

—ZIG ZIGLAR, MOTIVATIONAL SPEAKER

2.

FOCUS YOUR EXPECTATIONS

"I'm a great believer in luck and I find the harder I work,
the more I have of it."
-THOMAS JEFFERSON, STATESMAN

Go With What You Know

THERE are many reasons why people start businesses. Some are driven by an irresistible passion or calling. Others do so because they see a need in the marketplace and have found a way to satisfy the need. Still others go into business because they have a skill or special knowledge in a particular industry and want to sell this skill on the open market and in their own way. There are still other reasons why people become entrepreneurs but within each of these reasons are probably as many motives as there are people who want to become entrepreneurs.

The difference between a reason and a motive is clear. A reason is an intellectual **justification**—an intellectual defense or explanation for a choice or action. A motive, on the other hand, is an emotional **incentive** to act. For example, one might justify the need for a new car based on the need to get to work, but the motive to buy a jaguar rather than a sedan is that the jaguar would make you look cool going to work. The motive for buying an SUV is that it would be more convenient for you to transport a large family to various activities. This motive could also be the justification for buying the SUV. Motives are important for forcing us to act but reasons are the ways we justify our actions, whether they correspond to our motives or not. Our motives are explained by reasons. Our reasons are the public statements we make about why we do things. Our true motives tend to stay hidden. So the only thing outsiders have to work with are reasons we give for acting.

The best indication of why people start businesses is the reason they give. There are many reasons people give for becoming entrepreneurs. With so many answers to the question, "Why did you start your business?" we are led to wonder whether some reasons are better than others. Do some of these reasons make it easier to succeed quickly? I have found that reasons will not tell us much because all of them are legitimate. Reasons just do not point to the basic causes of why businesses succeed or fail.

So one of the first things a prospective business owner should do is assess her knowledge, skills and experience to make sure she has a solid foundation to support her reasons and motives. But before we describe how to make this assessment, we should define the terms we are using and understand how they interrelate and affect our chances of success. So, let's define "reasons" and "motives" in more detail.

Reasons are the thought processes we use to make decisions or arrive at conclusions. These thought processes analyze the facts that we have and form the basis of our conclusions. For example, John wants to open an accounting firm. He might combine the facts that he has 1) done well in math while in school, 2) has great organizing skills, 3) has $500 to invest in a business, and, 4) has access to a low-rate office space for rent. His conclusion is that he should start an accounting business. On the other hand, Mary decides she should open a restaurant because she 1) graduated from culinary school, 2) worked for three years as a chef under a boss with whom she couldn't get along, and 3) has friends who tells her that she can be a success. In both cases, these prospective entrepreneurs might conclude that they should start businesses.

Yet, most of our decisions are not certain because they are based on incorrect or incomplete information. If this is the case, can our decisions be better than the facts we use to make them? Not unless we want to rely on luck.

Motives, unlike reasons, are the emotions that create our desires. Some typical motives that lead us to make business decisions are pride, frustration, desire for recognition, desire for wealth, selfishness, greed, selflessness (wanting to give to others), confidence, etc. These are all emotional.

You should recognize two things about the relationship between reasons and motives because these principles are the basis of effective advertising as well. First, all reasons are accompanied by emotions, strong or mild. Second, only motives cause us to act, reasons don't. However, we justify our motives with reasons, real or imagined. For example, there are people who know every fact about the dangers of smoking and they still smoke. The reason they continue to send themselves to an early grave is because they don't have the desire or motive to change. On the other hand, we might know of someone who has a thousand shoes in her closet. Certainly there is no NEED for this many shoes but if you ask her why she has so many, she will come up with many cogent reasons why; for example, she found good bargains, she is really hard on shoes and they last longer when she only wears a pair once a year, or that since she is a person in the public eye, her reputation will suffer if others see her wearing the same pair twice.

The cause of many of our business problems boil down to making judgments on faulty or missing facts, accompanied by unjustified emotions or motives. When we don't realize how reasons and motives interact and influence our decisions, we run the risk of making the same mistakes repeatedly or not being able to jump out of a cycle of failure.

So, how do we avoid this trap that can slow down or derail our success? The answer is not as difficult as it seems.

Recognize What You Don't Know

Whether you have not yet started your business or whether you already are in business, stop now and assess your knowledge of your sales items, the industry, your craft, and your abilities. There are many sources of information at your fingertips to help you make this assessment. Association journals and college syllabi will give you an idea of the kinds of knowledge you will need to be competent in your field.

The same goes for finding out the business knowledge requirements for making, selling and delivering your services or merchandise. Look at the business programs that they offer and note the different types of courses required to have a well-rounded knowledge of business. Make a list of these knowledge areas and learn everything you can about them. You may take the courses for credit or not for credit.

Outside the formal academic environment, there are other sources of information. Your local Small Business Administration (SBA) office may offer seminars and workshops on various aspects of running a business. These offices will also be able to direct you to other organizations that offer these same types of programs.

Minimize The Surprises

However, all of the intellectual information in the world cannot substitute for experience gained through practice. So, if you have not yet started your business, you should get some experience under your belt before seriously considering putting all of your efforts into the startup right away. There is no better way to get this experience than by working or interning in the industry at several operational and management levels in a business of your selected industry.

This tactic might be impractical if your deadline for starting your business is too close. You may not have the time to expand your knowledge base through this type of experience. In this case, you can use the experience of others to gain the same type of expertise you need.

In the case where you cannot gain first-hand experience, you should create a team of advisors and mentors to help guide your growth. There are many sources of these helpful teammates available to you at little to no cost. The first source I recommend you approach is the group of business owners in your field or in similar industries. Make personal connections with them. People love to give advice and many welcome the chance to mentor new business owners. Invite them to coffee or lunch and tell them that you would like to bounce ideas off them or that you would like them to give you a reality check on your plans. While doing this, consider ways you can benefit them in return. This might be as simple as treating them to a periodic meal as you discuss your issues. You might decide to give them a monetary gift or retainer. The point is that you should never expect to get something for nothing.

Please note you're not forming a board of directors. This is a panel of advisors. Boards of directors are legal entities that are required of corporations. The members of boards have fiduciary responsibilities to the owners or stockholders of the business. Advisors don't have this legal obligation. Therefore, you should be careful to select advisors who are qualified to advise you on the area in which you need help. Selecting advisors merely because you like them or they are your friends might be dangerous because their opinions are only as good as their knowledge base.

To more clearly illustrate the difference between a panel of advisors and a board of directors, remember this. Some managers of corporations rely on advice from advisors and, direction from their board.

How many advisors should you have? Whom should you select as an advisor? The choice is up to you. You may select as many advisors, as you would like. You should select individuals with different skills, experiences and knowledge. They should be people who will tell you when your ideas are faulty as well as when you are right. Advisors are your trusted agents—your business friends.

You may select them from among your family members, social friends, business colleagues and associates, or professional service providers (e.g., bankers, accountants, financial planners, etc.) in or outside your community.

The key recommendation here is to avoid trying to go it alone. Take advantage of the help that is available. If you don't, your decisions will be more difficult to make and you will probably make the right decisions more slowly or less often.

Key Points

1. Assess your reasons and motives for starting a business. Make sure your motives are supported with good reasons.
2. List your business skills and weaknesses. Create a plan to minimize your weaknesses and to maximize your skills.
3. Gain practical experience in the industry, learning as much as you can about the inner workings of the business.
4. Create an alliance of trusted advisors to help scrutinize your ideas.
5. Seek help from all available sources.

"To win without risk is to triumph without glory."
–PIERRE CORNEILLE, POET

3.

FIND A DESIRE TO FIND A CLIENT

"People don't buy for logical reasons. They buy for emotional reasons."
"Every sale has five basic obstacles: no need, no money,
no hurry, no desire, no trust."

—ZIG ZIGLAR, MOTIVATIONAL SPEAKER

MORE businesses fail or fail to reach their profit goals by ignoring the basic rule of marketing. They fail, at the outset, to find out whether anyone wants what they are selling. There is no excuse for not getting this information because it is so easy to acquire. The problem is, however, we think that market research is as difficult to do as rocket science. It is not.

Too many business owners go into business without doing the most basic homework that tells them whether their idea is potentially profitable. They have a passion or desire to sell something they believe is very exciting. They assume others have this same passion to buy it. However, they do not test their passion in the marketplace to determine whether there are potential buyers out there, before starting a business. The faulty sequence of creating an idea then immediately creating a business to sell that product or service has doomed many businesses from the very beginning.

Finding the Market

One of the most important actions you can take to improve your chances for success is to identify your market. Your market is nothing more or less than that group of people who might buy what you're selling. They are the people who have a need or a desire for what you have to sell. Don't be fooled into thinking that everyone is your market. Not everyone will want what you're selling. Not everyone needs what you're selling. Not everyone who needs what you're selling wants what you're selling. Not everyone who wants what you're selling will want to buy it from you. Not everyone who will want to buy from you will be able to buy from you. Your role is to convert the people with needs and wants into your clients. You must first find them before you can convince them to buy.

Let's look at the first group you should identify in the category of "your market." This group has a need for your product or service. This is your primary market. If you're able to convince anyone to buy from you, the first people you should approach are these people who have a need. Don't waste your time, money, and effort on people who have no need or desire for what you're selling. Where's the sense in trying to sell diapers to people who have no babies? Why should you waste your money trying to sell cigarettes to nonsmokers? Yet, many naïve business owners do this by targeting their message to those who definitely will not buy what they're selling. If you have the attitude that "Everyone is my market," you will waste your time and money trying to talk to everyone. Your advertising campaign will not be focused. It will be too broad because you will try to make it big enough to address as many people as possible. So the bottom line is, you should try to find those with a need and talk directly to this need in your ads. Place your ads only where you are likely to find these people.

The second group you should identify is the group that wants to buy what you're selling. There are people who have a need (or perceived need) for what you're selling. They must be convinced that they can get it from you and should buy it from you. There are others in this group who might not know that you're selling what they need. You have to let them know that what you're selling can satisfy their need or desire. But more importantly, you need to convince them that what you're selling can satisfy their needs better than anyone else who is also selling what you're selling. So, you have to convert those people with the need into interested prospects. Through your advertising and promotional campaigns, you make it possible to turn <u>possible</u> clients into <u>probable</u> clients. The focus of your advertising is not to convince them that they need what you're selling. The focus is to distinguish yourself as the very best provider of that product or service.

Finally, when your prospects are aware that you can meet their needs, you have one more step to take. It is now your responsibility to make them take the step of buying from you. This can only be done if you present your offering at a price they are willing and able to pay. So the value you're able to associate with it as well as the price you charge for it become the primary considerations at this point. If your product or service only represents limited value in the mind of the potential buyer, you will have to limit the price you charge. If the value is very high, you may attach a higher price. This entire process is focused on finding out how the potential client defines value and translating that value into a monetary amount that you will charge. This amount can be more than others charge, less than others charge, or somewhere in the middle. There are two easy ways of making this decision. You may create a market study and ask potential buyers what they would pay for it or you may test different prices in different markets with similar demographics.

This lesson was demonstrated when I was selling a premium service to clients in the resort areas of Colorado. After looking at the returns on our various services, we decided to drop a service that was providing a relatively low profit margin. My plan was to double the price of the service and wait for our clients to drop off. Well, although there was a flood of complaints, only one client out of over 350 dropped the service. Having failed at this attempt to phase out this service through attrition, I increased the rates of the service another 100% within that same month. Again, there was the predictable flood of complaints but only two clients dropped the service this time. My conclusion was that the clients placed such a high value on the service that they would have continued to pay whatever we asked. In the end, I had the staff call the clients to tell them we were no longer offering the service. We recommended several of our competitors to them for the service. The lesson in this experience is that the clients valued the service so highly that they were apparently willing to pay whatever we asked. So, value was not a function of price but, of perceived benefit.

The Market Study

The primary purpose of any business should be to find its primary market—the group that needs and wants what you sell. Identifying this group must be more than a wish or desire to have certain people buy our offerings. This identification must be based on data that we collect in the marketplace.

For example, let's assume we want to sell memberships in a new Internet social network that is designed to connect alumni of weight loss summer camps. We could spend thousands of dollars designing a system that provides many features similar to *Facebook* and *MySpace*. Since these sites are so popular and growing rapidly, we think there is no way of failing. When we try to sell memberships, however, we get no buyers. What has happened? You did what many entrepreneurs do. You fell in love with your idea and believe others would. You failed to ask the campers if they want to maintain the relationships with their fellow campers. Moreover, you failed to learn that the participants hated the camp and didn't want to be reminded of the experience after leaving. You didn't ask and didn't learn that there is no market for what you're selling. You could have avoided this problem with a simple questionnaire that would give you the answers you need even though they are not the answers you want or expect.

Most entrepreneurs panic when bankers and investors talk of needing a market study. They believe they should embark on a complicated process that involves complex statistics and mathematical computations to find out exactly how well the product or service will sell. This is not the case!

A market study can be as simple as creating a small questionnaire and asking for the opinions of friends, acquaintances and passersby. The survey does not have to be longer than a handful of questions. However, it can be as long or short as necessary to get the information you need from the people who matter. Go to www.AskJerry-TheFixer.com to get a sample market survey. This survey will give you an idea of how simple a study can be while providing valuable data to help you find business. Unless you have a strong need to contact respondents, make your questionnaires anonymous.

Once you have the data from the survey, you need to translate those data into information. You must determine what the respondents are telling you and why they are saying it. Only when you take this final step will you make sense of the data and be able to make the right judgments based on the information the data give you.

What A Market Study Provides

Market studies can help you in more ways than by simply giving you a go or no-go decision on starting your business. A market study can answer any question you might have about every aspect of running your business. For example, before starting your business, you should want to find out the answers to the following questions.

Is there a need for my product or service?
Where is that need located?
How big is that need?
Will people pay the asking price?
How much are they willing to pay?
How can I make my offering more attractive?
Can I create a successful business?
How can I make a recurring income from my clients?

You need to ask these questions in order to make a logical go or no-go decision on whether to start the business. You cannot answer these questions alone or in a vacuum. You need to get these answers from others. Those who can give you some of the answers are your potential clients and colleagues. You can also get helpful answers from researching the industry and the demographic area where you intend to do business.

After you have started your company, you should continue to perform market studies if you are to succeed quickly and unequivocally. These ongoing, periodic market studies are nothing more than surveys. Therefore, you should continue to poll your clients, former clients, prospective clients and professional colleagues. Of course, the questions will be different because you will be seeking different information, for the most part. So, your questions will include these.

How am I doing?
Am I taking care of your needs adequately?
Am I providing the right services and products you want and need?

How is the after-sales service?
What am I doing right?
What improvements would you like to see?
What other products or services would you buy?
What does this ad say to you?
How effective is this ad?
How well are our employees performing?
Do we need to hire more employees?

The market study is an ideal source of free or low-cost advice. It allows you to test your ideas and plans before rashly committing funds. It is an essential tool to guide your management decisions. You should use it regularly. However, many struggling entrepreneurs do not take the time to administer surveys and end up wasting time and money on missteps.

I often ask business owners if they are surveying their clients and, invariably, they proudly answer that they do it all the time. When I ask them to show me their results, however, they have to admit, sheepishly, that they only take these surveys orally. The results are in their heads. They claim to ask all of their customers whether the customers liked the service they received or ask the customers what other products or services they would like to buy. If they are not being disingenuous, then they are wasting their time.

First, I would be willing to bet that these owners are not even asking the questions. Second, if they are, then what they are hearing is meaningless because the only information that's in their heads is the last bit of data they receive. The only way to take a helpful and authentic survey is to record the results on paper or electronically and evaluate them objectively.

One practice you should NOT adopt is that of taking surveys in your head. Why is this method flawed? This practice is about as effective as not surveying at all. There is no effective way of measuring data that is in your head because, as the data change, your judgments change. You have no baseline to start a measurement and no way to make valid judgments because all you have are the latest impressions that might be colored by your assumptions, emotions, and desires. When you make an effort to record these data, they do not change. You can, then, go back and make accurate measurements of the information you receive and any changes that occur over time based on additional or new data that comes in.

An example of how we distort impressions is seen in the way most of us will hear a statement made by one or two people and then we automatically report that "most people believe…." One or two statements will never add up to "most people" or even "many people" and this assumption will take on a life of its own until some intelligent listener questions it. So if you want to make accurate decisions and if you want those decisions to have the desired effect of increasing income, you must record your surveys by having your targets fill out a written survey or by physically recording the answers to your oral questions as you receive them.

Market studies and surveys are crucial tools in creating a successful business and in continually improving the business you have. Without these, you are left to rely on guesses and trial-and-error. This is the most inefficient means of making business decisions.

Later in this book (Chapter 9), we will talk more about the need and benefits of having advisors. I suggest that we look upon surveys as a tool for converting your clients into external advisors. After all, they should be the focus of everything you do in business because if you aren't satisfying their needs and desires, you will never succeed.

So if you are thinking of opening a tennis shop because you

love tennis or opening a restaurant because you host such great dinner parties, stop! Go through the following checklist before you invest a dime:

1. Ask friends and colleagues what they think of your business idea. Do not keep your idea a secret. There is hardly a business idea that has not been tried and if you're doing something totally new, you should think carefully about whether there is even a market for it.
   a. Ask them to be brutally honest.
   b. Record the feedback they give you and evaluate the types and frequencies of answers you get.
   c. Then evaluate your results.
2. Look at the marketplace and evaluate similar businesses.
   a. Determine how successful they are and why they are successful.
   b. Record how many of these businesses there are and note the features of each: Location, items they sell, size, number of employees, etc.
   c. Group these potential competitors to see if there are similarities that will help you find a reason why some are more successful than others.
3. Take a critical look at how much you really know about the business and industry, in which you want to get involved.
   a. Do you have practical, real-world experience?
   b. Note all of your strengths and weaknesses in two columns.
   c. Identify ways to capitalize on your strengths and actions you can take to turn the weaknesses around and create strengths.
4. Do your research. How big, exactly, is your target market?
   a. How stable is that market?
   b. Where do they live?

    c. What do they buy most often?

    d. How often do they make the purchases?

If the results of the above assessment don't look positive, put profits before passion and look for another business opportunity.

Key Points

1. Define your primary market. Realize that not everyone fits into this category. Make your primary market as narrow as possible for quick success.
2. Don't ignore what the market wants. Find out what it is and resolve to make it a priority to satisfy that need, desire, or expectation. This is your reason for being in business.
3. Create simple, written market studies and use them frequently to ensure your business remains on track.
4. Frequent and continuing market research is the key to business success.

"Research is formalized curiosity. It is poking and prying with a purpose."

—ZORA NEALE HURSTON, ANTHROPOLOGIST

4.

SPECIALIZE TO FIND A NICHE

*"The jack-of-all-trades seldom is good at any. Concentrate
all of your efforts on one definite chief aim."*
—NAPOLEON HILL, SUCCESS COACH

ONE of the most difficult concepts for inexperienced business
owners to grasp is that when you try to be all things to all
people, you have abandoned a shortcut to success. Many mistakenly
believe that the more variety of goods and services they offer the
marketplace, the more clients they will be able to attract. Nothing
can be further from the truth for new or smaller businesses. In
fact, if you want to become successful quickly, you need to focus
and specialize on a narrow market. When you devote the time
and money on attracting a narrower clientele, you will actually
save money by presenting a stronger sales message to the most
responsive group—the group that is more likely to buy from you.

It has been proven, time after time, that when you specialize,
your chances of quicker success will improve dramatically. So,
instead of creating a retail store, you should consider creating
a clothing store. And an even better idea is to create a men's or
women's clothing store.

There are two major reasons why such specialization is
preferable. Both reasons have to do with effective marketing. The
first reason relates to the cost of marketing. The second reason
relates to the quality of the advertising you are able to deliver to
the marketplace.

Marketing Costs

It is especially critical in the early stages of a business that you diligently control costs. Many businesses fail in their early years because they do not have enough money to carry on operations until business grows sufficiently. Some start out with an overly optimistic expectation that they will succeed quickly. So, they start out with just enough capital to meet these expectations. When this capital is not enough to carry the business through the lean years of slower growth, the business fails due to capital anemia. Other businesses start out with sufficient capital to fund operations but find that their marketing efforts are not as effective as the owners thought they would be. So, the owner runs out of funds to support more marketing and operations.

Both of these situations suggest that whatever funds you have available to grow your business should be spent sparingly and carefully. You should spend only enough in marketing to get your point across to those most likely to buy from you. So, the more narrowly you identify your target market—those who are most likely to buy what you're offering—the less money you will spend on those who are not likely to buy. It stands to reason, then, that the more you narrow your offerings, the smaller your target market will be. Having a smaller target market is desirable when that market is large enough to support your business. With a more focused target market, you will be better able to speak directly and more clearly to the needs and desires of this group. Every dollar, therefore, will have a bigger return.

In summary, the smaller your audience, the fewer places you will have to place your advertising message to reach them and the less it will cost to market to the audience.

Marketing Accuracy

Another important benefit of specializing is that specialization reduces the number of messages you'll have to create to sell your offerings. The reason for this reduction, again, is that fewer offerings narrow your target market. The narrower the target market, the fewer needs and benefits you will have to address.

The best messages you can deliver to potential buyers are those messages that talk their language—that meet their specific needs and desires. The best messages are those that speak directly to their needs, their experiences, their desires, and their interests. The more audiences you have, the more sales messages you will have to create and the more advertising campaigns you will have to develop in order to do this well. It costs money to create many advertising messages and there is no guarantee that you will get the right message for all of your niche markets. It will be difficult enough for you to create the right message when you have even one target or niche. The difficulty expands when you have several markets.

For example, it will be difficult enough to try to sell the same product (pain medication, for example) to teens and the elderly. You might consider advertising your product by showing how well it relieves pain from sports injuries or how well it relieves arthritis pain. If you create an ad that focuses on relieving pain that results from sports trauma, you will address the interests of the teens. If your ad focuses on relieving the pain of arthritis, you will primarily address the interests of the elderly. To speak to both groups effectively, you need to create two ads.

Whenever you select one audience (called the "market") over another, you will be able to create a very strong appeal to the selected group. If, on the other hand, you decide to create a message that does not address the needs of either group, your advertising will be weak and not address the needs of either. You will waste money with your weak advertising message. However, if you switch messages between these two groups, you will be able to create strong advertising appeals to both groups. However, this will cost you more to do because you will have to create several advertising campaigns.

In short, these markets are so different, that you will find yourself switching back and forth between two messages or you will revert to trying to speak to both at the same time and you will end up creating a weak appeal to both groups. Think of all the time and money that will be wasted on unclear messages! However, if you choose to sell a product that is best suited to one or the other, you will be able to concentrate on making the strongest argument possible to that one group. All of your creative ideas for attracting that one group will be much more effective and efficiently created.

Here's a personal example. As a business mentor, I can advertise my services to all small businesses within my market area. However, I choose to target only start-up companies. By doing this, I can create a very strong appeal to this segment of the business population by describing how I can serve their needs, which are different from the needs of established businesses. Consequently, my advertising message is more focused and stronger. I spend a lot less money attracting this smaller market than I would spend trying to address the needs of all small businesses. Moreover, even though I target a small section of this broad business population, I have clients that range from startups to growing and established businesses because I don't limit my clientele to only startups. I focus on a few but I accept everyone who wants my services.

The biggest fear of new business owners in adopting this success strategy is the fear that they will have to limit their clients to only those they target. This is not true! Focusing does not imply you will have to exclude any business or limit your scope of business.

Focusing on the teen market does not mean you cannot do business with the elderly. You will accept the patronage of anyone and everyone who wants to do business with you. You will simply choose to spend your money wisely to lure the largest, group that is likely to buy from you.

Embrace Your Difference

The key to fast entrepreneurial success is to set your business apart in the market. Being different is good. Being in the middle of the pack is bad. Being safe is accepting mediocrity. Taking risk is making a bold statement that people will notice.

I once suggested that an accountant name her business *Accounting Magic*. She thought it was a terrible name because no accountant would select a name like that. It suggested that she didn't take her clients' business seriously, she claimed. When I presented this name to a very successful businessperson who had proven her excellent marketing skills, her reaction was the exact opposite. "That's fantastic!" she exclaimed. She thought the name would stand out and be noticed by potential clients. This is the name of the game, to be noticed. Being different and being willing to change the image of the stodgy accountant who sits in a dark room like Ebenezer Scrooge just might give you the opportunity to make a bold statement in the marketplace.

Embracing change and thriving on forward movement is the key to growth in size and profits. Quiznos is a company that has proven these maxims over the years. Their advertisements have been annoying, unintelligible, and, even repulsive, at times. Yet, this company has made a name for itself by emphasizing the difference between itself, Subway, McDonald's and every other sandwich shop in the marketplace. In fact, the ranking of Quiznos among all sandwich shops went from number 15 in 2002 to number three in 2006. This doesn't mean that only

the advertising rocketed Quiznos to the top and this doesn't mean that advertising will keep it near the top. Backing up that advertising with performance is also necessary. The only point I'm making is that daring to be different contributed to its meteoric success.

The attitude you should adopt in reference to your competition is "I am better because I'm different." Don't be the accountant who has to conform to the image of the staid, somber, boring bean counter. Be the one who demonstrates the dynamism of your profession. Be the one who demonstrates that financial books and numbers are fun and exciting. Resolve to create this attitude in your clients and potential clients.

I must give you a word of caution, however. In your enthusiasm to show your difference—your Unique Selling Proposition (USP), be mindful that your USP should complement the market's expectations and not challenge them. In some instances, Quiznos might have been accused of potentially turning off sandwich buyers by walking the tightrope of good taste versus being on the edge. The accountant who claims she can make numbers say anything is a lot more dangerous than the one who says she creates magic with numbers. The retailer who says no one can beat his prices is a lot safer than the one who says he will do anything to get your business (including lie?).

Create Your Niche

Sometimes, finding your niche means creating your niche. If, through your creativity, you can see a need that no one else sees or if you see a need in a different way than others have, don't be afraid to accept your role of exposing that need and satisfying it in your own unique manner. Sometimes needs arise out of desires or conveniences. The history of marketing is full of examples where conveniences become needs. One example

is the cup holder in personal vehicles. Now everyone expects to have them in the vehicles they buy. Another example is the phenomenon of Cabbage Patch Dolls. In fact, many toys (for kids and grownups) are marketed as needs, quite successfully. Ask yourself whether what you sell can be marketed as a need. Perhaps it is a special membership category or special services for your clients.

Thinking outside the box can be fearful, but it is sure to be liberating. It can open you to a world that is bigger than the one you have always experienced. The crucial benefit of putting yourself in this different situation, however, is that it gives you the opportunity to be viewed differently by others. If done correctly, it will give you the distinction of being, not the first one people think of to buy what you're selling, but the ONLY one people think of.

Creating a profitable market share entails specializing—not trying to be all things to all people. It requires that you implement, not all of your ideas, but only your best one at a time and push your message about it heavily and consistently. In other words, concentrate on being a serial specialist.

Key Points

1. Specialization is good and is more desirable than being a generalist in business.
2. When you specialize, you save money and resources by focusing on a specialized market.
3. Every business has to market in order to be successful. When a business can limit the range of marketing messages it needs to create, it operates more efficiently
4. Specialization implies being different and owners should embrace and promote specialization of the company if the company is to be successful more quickly.

5. Being different in business is a good thing if it translates into identifying your USP, which is the key to market dominance.

"Hardly any human being is capable of pursuing two professions or two arts rightly."

—PLATO, PHILOSOPHER

5.

CREATE A CONSISTENT BRAND

"You now have to decide what 'image' you want for your brand.
Image means personality. Products, like people, have personalities,
and they can make or break them in the market place."

—DAVID OGILVY

Your brand is your exclusive business identity to the world. It must be protected zealously, guarded jealously, and promoted relentlessly. It is all that your business has to distinguish itself from other businesses that are similar to it. Since most new business owners do not realize the importance of the brand, businesses fail from lack of having a clear identity. Your identity, in major part, can draw clients and customers to you.

Every crucial business activity an owner performs falls under the umbrella of marketing. We cannot say this enough. When you engage in creating a strong attraction for potential and actual clients, you are engaged in the marketing activity of branding. When you are protecting the identity of the business or its products or services, this is also branding.

In this chapter, we will explore both aspects of branding and demonstrate the steps you should take in creating a strong, recognizable brand that will set you apart from all competitors in your market. We hope that you will not fall into the trap that many struggling business owners fall into of having their brand created for them rather than creating the brand that reflects their vision.

Without having a clear and unique brand, you will suffer the plight of many businesses that never stand out in the crowd. You remain simply one in the pack and clients will find it difficult to understand why they should buy from you rather than from company X. Without a strong brand, it will take you longer to create the large clientele that will help you achieve or surpass your business goals.

The Attractive Power of Branding

Branding is the process of creating a clear identity for your business. When that identity is linked to excellence in your field, you will stand out as the best in what you do. You will stand out far above everyone else who claims to do what you do. And when the public can easily recognize that brand, your business will flourish.

Branding is like a magnet in that proper branding draws clients to you with an invisible force that they cannot resist. But *proper* branding doesn't just happen by accident or on its own. In creating a brand for your business, you must present a clear and consistent image of your business' identity, then manage that image so that people get the message you want them to get each time they see it.

Creating and managing a brand are straightforward processes that not many independent business owners know how to do. What follow are explanations of the components of branding.

Branding Components

The components of a business the owner is able to brand are the **purpose, name, logo, icon, slogan, color scheme**, and **theme music.**

The first branding decision you make about the prospective business is your **purpose** or mission. Ideally, you want to engage in an enterprise that is different and better than anything else in the marketplace.

You want to distinguish what you do from every other business in your industry. In order to do this effectively, you must create a clear, specific and focused description of what you do to express this distinction. In defining your business, you would help yourself greatly by limiting the range of your business (as discussed in the previous chapter). So, Instead of opening a clothing store, it is better to start with a maternity clothing store or children's clothing store. Instead of selling hand tools, start by selling carpentry or automotive tools.

After limiting the range of your business, you must describe your purpose in a way that states how you are different and better than any other business that does what you do. Your goal is to tell the market that you are not just the best source of what you sell, but also the only logical source for them.

After identifying a product or service to sell, the next decision about the business identity an entrepreneur makes is what to call the business, the **name**. This step might not take place if one buys into a franchise. Deciding on a name is critical because everyone will refer to your business and distinguish it from others by this name. You don't want any confusion here. The name you choose must reflect the image you want to plant in people's heads when they hear the name. The name can be fun, playful and exciting, such as *Yahoo!* or *Google* ™. On the other hand, it can be very serious and no-nonsense such as *National Business Machines* or *First Bank of Bugtussle*.

The prolific writer-producer, Tyler Perry demonstrates an effective branding technique by including his name in the title of every play, TV, show or movie he creates. His reason is to distinguish his works from other comedies and to give the audience an indication of what they can expect before they even watch his works. So, he brands his work with his personal name. I have used this technique to help clients brand their services. For example, there are the *Pochop Health Assurance System* and the *Pochop Vitality Optimizer* to identify two unique medical services offered by Dr. Pochop.

When choosing a name, you have many options. Some options are, generally, better or stronger than others. In order of increasing impact, the business name might reflect your own name (*Jim Kale Insurance*), your location (*Dallas Insurance Co.*), nothing in particular (*Priam Insurance*), your product or service (*The Insurance Center*), or the benefits you provide (*Peace Of Mind Life Insurance*). You might have good reasons for selecting any of these as a basis for your name. For example, even though using your own name ranks relatively low on the scale for impact, your name might have the strong impact that a name such as "Trump" has and it makes that decision to use your name a no-brainer. In any event, you have to think ahead a bit and anticipate whether that name will complement all of the other elements of branding and not clash with any of them. Additionally, the name should be memorable, easily pronounceable, short, and different.

The next element we will consider is the **logo**. Your logo might leave an even bigger impression on people's minds than does the name since your logo can be viewed more frequently than your name will be heard. This all depends on your advertising strategy. It might also depend on how closely your logo reflects or represents your name. To see examples of this, go to www.AskJerry-TheFixer. com. See the examples of the Coca-Cola, Bennigan's and McDonald's logos. These logos clearly represent the names of the companies.

The logo is a purely visual symbol of your business. Therefore, in selecting or designing a logo, you must pay attention to those visual characteristics such as size, color, shape or pattern, and depth. Depth refers to how the logo appears in one, two or three dimensions. Your logo should be designed so that it is simple, scalable, attractive and not repulsive, distinctive and noticeable. Compare the examples at www.AskJerry-TheFixer.com at Figure 2. From left to right they become simpler, more easily scalable, and easily modifiable by a competitor to get around copyright infringement laws. The Nike logo is much stronger than the others because it is simpler.

In the case of the Starbucks logo, many coffee houses have developed similar logos by changing just enough of the Starbucks details that the courts have judged them to be sufficiently different that they are not violating Starbucks' copyright.

The simpler the design is, the more scalable it will be without losing detail, no matter how large or small it is reproduced. The simpler it is, the more easily you can protect it from being copied or modified by the competition.

The colors must be such that they do not clash with other colors in your company's color scheme or be overshadowed when placed next to other colors in logos, pictures or ads.

A client of mine that sold water systems created their own full-color ads for local newspapers. One day, at their office, I finished reading the newspaper and one of the owners asked how I liked the ad. I had to admit that I did not see it and I carefully searched through the newspaper again for it. Again, I didn't see the ad and the owner had to point it out to me. The problem was that the ad was created in sky blue to represent the water but it was surrounded by ads featuring bold yellows, reds and blacks. These other colors completely obscured the pale blue of their ad and I totally missed it.

Since colors convey positive and negative feelings, you should choose those colors that call out the most positive feelings. Moreover, if more than one color is used, there should be no more than two in your design and they should not clash with each other.

Another important element of branding your business is the **icon** to symbolize what you do. An icon is a graphical image that symbolizes a concept.

Icons are different from slogans in that they are not words. They are different from logos in that they are not static visual symbols. All icons are mobile even though they do not move. For example, the Travelocity gnome, which is a statue, gets around. And Betty Crocker, who is generally recognized by only her picture, gives advice over the phone and signs responses to her customers (http://chnm.gmu.edu/features/sidelights/crocker.html). Icons have human characteristics such as speech or pantomime, thought, dress, movement, and human form. They also symbolize something beyond what they signify. This symbolization is an important concept because the symbol expresses the benefit you want to stress. For example, Smokey Bear symbolizes safety, Geoffrey Giraffe symbolizes the fun of Toys"R"Us, Ronald McDonald along with the associated residents of McDonaldland visually represent fun as his slogan states ("In Any Language He Means 'Fun!'"), and Speedy of Alka Seltzer fame symbolizes quick action.

Geoffrey Giraffe is described by www.tvacres.com/ in this way.

> Geoffrey Giraffe - Spokes-animal for the "Toys 'R Us" nationwide chain-store. Geoffrey began appearing on TV in the early 1970s plugging children's toys in anticipation of the Christmas rush. An actor who wears a two-legged giraffe costume with a seven-feet-tall neck brings Geoffrey's character to life. In recent years, he teamed with such new characters as Gigi, his wife; Baby Gee, his daughter; and his son, Junior. Geoffrey and family don't sell particular products

but only represent the store as a whole. Neither do the characters talk. They only pantomime their commercial roles. Charles Lazarus founded Toys 'R Us when he returned home from World War II where he had served as a cryptologist. His store was originally called "Children's Supermart. The R's [Sic.} in his company name were reversed to increase recognition of his store. He later changed the store's name to Toys 'R Us, keeping the letter "R" reversed. Toys 'R Us carries all major toy lines including those manufactured by Hasbro, Mattel, Coleco Industries, Kenner/Parker Brother Toys and Fischer Price Toys. The new animatronic Geoffrey, created by legendary movie creature expert Stan Winston, features the "distinctive, witty voice" of Jim Hanks, brother of actor Tom Hanks.

Most businesses do not have icons and probably do not suffer from not having one. However, some businesses have very recognizable icons that instantly symbolize what they do and how well they do it. Take, for example, the Travelocity traveling gnome or the Geico gecko or cavemen. These icons instantly conjure up the core benefits of the companies even though one of them does this by emphasis on what the business is not—a gecko.

The **slogan**, like your business name, is the verbal representation of your business or what you sell. Similar to your name, your slogan should be easily pronounceable, short, and memorable. Your slogan can express a feature of your business or a benefit you provide. A feature is a characteristic of your business that tells what the business is or what it does. A benefit, on the other hand, tells what good you provide to your clients. It says how you will satisfy their needs or wants. Since people only buy because of what benefits they get, your slogan should, ideally, express a benefit rather than a feature.

The slogan should also be memorable. Therefore, you should attempt to create one that is short. If it is not short, it should be easily pronounceable. If it flows from the tongue quickly, that's a good feature. If you are able to connect the slogan to your name and a benefit in one breath, the more powerful it will be. Consider these slogans.

"Winston Tastes Good, Like a Cigarette Should"
"How Do You Spell Relief?"
"You're In Safe Hands"
"That Was Easy!"
"Chase What Matters"
"We Try Harder"

I have attempted to prioritize them in descending order of effectiveness or strength. The first, even though it is the longest, is still easy to say. Its strengths are in the use of the product name and its emphasis on its core benefit, good taste. The second slogan focuses on the benefit of providing relief but it uses a very creative ploy to associate relief with "Rolaids." The third slogan is short and directly states the benefit of safety. But it doesn't include the name of the product. The third is less strong because, even though it stresses a benefit of ease, it is not associated directly with a company or product and the subject, "That," is too vague to associate with anything on its own. "Chase what matters" is a play on the name of Chase Bank in 2008 by the JP Morgan Chase & Co. but the benefit of what matters is too vague to relate to anything in particular. If you go to the chase what matters website (www.chasewhatmatters.com), you are greeted with a list of things that matter but the list seems artificial. The list includes protection, complete control, rewards for being you, 24-7, and more value. I doubt that several of these are even benefits to most people and the list looks forced. Perhaps this is why the slogan is not on the Chase or JP Morgan sites even though the company paid $70M to promote it over three months. Finally, "We try harder" is well recognized and short but it doesn't specify the business or the benefit. It is a negative feature that Avis used to promise they work hard. Apparently, the wide use of the phrase in advertising and its age has helped it to be easily recognizable.

Color plays a very important role in evoking the feelings of people. Certain colors, even in our daily language, leave important feelings in one's mind (e. g., a black lie, a grey day, feeling blue). So, the **color scheme** of your business is an important element of branding. It can be used to evoke feelings of attraction or to distinguish your business from your competitors' businesses. A business that has a distinctive and recognizable color scheme will have a bigger impact in the market than one that uses inconsistent color schemes to display its logo, name, and icon.

When choosing the color scheme, you should consider the industry you're in, what you sell, your name, icon, and location. The key to creating a balanced color scheme is coordination and simplicity. Since your color scheme should be reflected in your logo, it shouldn't be too complex or based on too many hues. Normally two hues are plenty.

Make sure that the hues do not clash as backgrounds to different font colors. For example, a web site with grey letters on a black background is much harder to read than one with white or yellow letters on a black background. Undoubtedly, you will use your color scheme as a backdrop for messages such as your name, slogans, price lists, or other wording. If you can use the same font color against all hues of your color scheme, you will have a more consistent look and will have easier decisions to make.

For a more detailed guide on color meanings and a helpful guide for creating a coordinated branding campaign, read the comprehensive *Midas Branding Guide* at www.AskJerry-TheFixer. com.

Key Points

1. Your business' brand is its unique identity.
2. In the realm of marketing, your brand is as important and should be as unique as the Employer Identity Number (EIN) that the IRS uses to identify your company.
3. An effective brand identity attracts customers to your business.
4. When branding your company, you should consider the five senses and how your company makes an impression on each of the senses of the buying public.
5. Not every sense may play a role in the brand of your company or product. However, you should consider all of the senses to ensure that you do not overlook an important element of your brand.
6. The *Midas Branding Guide* is available for your use at www. AskJerry-TheFixer.com.

"Your premium brand had better be delivering something special, or it's not going to get the business."
—WARREN BUFFETT, VALUE INVESTOR

PLAN TO THE LEVEL OF YOUR NEEDS

"A goal without a plan is just a wish."
—ANONYMOUS

Create A Plan

NORMALLY, we panic when we hear the words "business planning." These words tend to make us think of a highly structured document that contains a lot of technical concepts about business that we will never use in the real world. We think of a plan as only a hoop the banker will require us to jump through if we want to qualify for a loan.

Nothing can be further from the truth. I often tell clients that even though they have enough money to start their businesses and don't need outside financing, they should create a plan. A plan is necessary because what's in their heads takes on a different character when they put it on paper and commit to a certain way of doing things.

When the ideas are on paper, they don't shift and change as they would if they were simply in your mind. What you have on paper is a foundation on which you can build your business. Once you write down all of these elements together, you can see, more easily, what fits together and what doesn't.

Often, entrepreneurs have very clear ideas of how they want to organize their businesses. The plans they have for each area of the business are soundly constructed. But when they put the sections together, they find that the whole works a lot differently than expected. Business planning students of mine will often change their original plans after seeing that the elements do not work together as they hoped. This is a valuable lesson because it saves precious time and money that would be wasted if these ideas were implemented.

As the business grows, a plan is helpful to visualize the changes that have to be made as obstacles arise during the course of doing business. The business plan is similar in some ways to a military battle plan. It is widely recognized that as soon as a military plan is implemented, it must be changed. This is true of a business plan as well. Does the fact that the plan changes mean that the plan is useless? This is not true, at all. Without a plan, one has no ideas of what steps to take and when to take them. Without a plan, there is no clear goal or list of the resources needed to achieve the goal. So planning is necessary and helpful in keeping the goal in focus and adjusting to the circumstances of your business.

Find a Logical Process

Planning helps businesses create a logical process for growth and development. This process might be sequential, chronological, or a combination of both. A sequential process of growth relies on making steps in an efficient order. For example, before you can hire an employee you must advertise the position then evaluate the applications, select the best applications for interviews, interview the applicants and select the best qualified. To alter this sequence makes no sense at all. It will probably result in making a blind decision. On the other hand, a chronological process of growth involves taking steps in the order of time. This process is represented when you create a goal that has a time deadline. Certain actions have to take place by given dates in order to ensure the deadline is met. For example, a plan to save money by putting aside a portion of your pay check each pay period relies on making deposits at given times rather than in any sequence. You can make the deposits at any time within the month and make as large or small a deposit as you want, as long as the deposits are made to get you to your goal.

The truth about business goals is that the vast majority will have elements of sequential and chronological steps. To the extent you can combine both in your plans, the more successful you will be in reaching your goals. So, let us explore how to correctly set goals.

Create Achievable Goals

A goal is simply an end result that you want to attain. It is more than a simple wish because every authentic goal has to incorporate a plan for achieving it. That being said, you should create attainable goals. Do not create goals that are beyond your capabilities and resources to accomplish. What follows is a helpful tool to help you create attainable goals.

Virtually every goal can be broken down into several action items that you need to perform in order to accomplish the goal. These component actions are called objectives and every goal must have at least two objectives. If a goal cannot be broken down into two or more objectives (steps in a process), it is simply an objective of a larger goal. So, goals comprise several actions.

Make a list of each action that you must accomplish, sequentially and chronologically, to accomplish the goal. By breaking down the goal into its component parts, you are making it more manageable.

Well-written goals and objectives have the same characteristics:

49

1. They have deadlines or ending dates;
2. They are written in complete sentences;
3. They use active verbs that are measurable or observable; and,
4. They are assigned to only one person who is responsible for seeing that it is accomplished.

The deadline is extremely important because if there were none, the action could be accomplished at any time or at no time. In every case of goal setting, you do not want the goal hanging out in an indeterminate future because it doesn't call for any action to be performed at any time. The deadline can either be a time or date when the action must be *completed* or a time when the action must *begin*. The deadline can never be identified as "ongoing" or "continuous" because these statements have as much force as having no time limit at all. Even for ongoing actions, we must identify times when they should be accomplished, for example, "The 1st of every month" or "Every Wednesday." Deadlines are essential for measuring when the action is complete whether the action is an objective toward a goal or the goal itself.

The next criterion for an objective or goal is that it must be stated in a complete sentence. For example the statement, "Hire three employees," is a complete sentence. It is clear what must be accomplished. On the other hand, "Employees" or "Three employees," are not sentences. They are not even complete thoughts. The reader—even if it is you—could interpret the incomplete phrases in many different ways. Does it mean you will evaluate three employees? Does it mean you will fire three employees? Does it mean you must assign work to three employees? It is conceivable that the meaning of incomplete phrases can be forgotten over time and you could waste time trying to reconstruct what was intended. So, you must always write goals and objectives with a subject, verb, and object.

Next, the verbs that you use should be measurable or observable. That is the only way you will be able to judge whether the action is accomplished and how well it is accomplished. A well written objective will state, "**List all** the tools needed for the job." The word "list" is an observable action verb. The word "all" is measurable. Once you produce this list, anyone can observe that the task was completed. On the other hand, the statement, "know what tools are necessary," is completely unverifiable. How would I be able to tell if anyone knew what tools are required? The only way this can be accomplished if by having them **list, say,** or **describe** the tools that are needed. Doing something active such as listing, describing or saying is the only way for me to verify that the knowledge is there. All active, action verbs are observable or measurable.

Finally, you should never make a group or several people responsible for getting a task accomplished. The reason for this is simple. When many people are given the responsibility, no one is given the responsibility. If, as the boss, you were to check up on the progress of the task or were to try to find out who failed to carry out the responsibility, you would be likely to be met with only finger pointing. Does that mean that the person who is assigned the responsibility must perform the actions? No. The responsible person can certainly delegate the task or portions of the task to specific individuals to accomplish. Delegation is a good practice that can extend to lower levels of the organization or it can be extended outside the organization. For example, if you give a manager the obligation to come up with a new sales contract, the proper thing for the manager to do is pass much of the work on to the company's legal advisor along with your desires for the characteristics the contract should have. So, while the manager is making sure it gets done, he or she does not, and should not, perform this task personally.

Make Forward Movement Each Day

Setting goals for each department or function of your company is the fastest way to achieve success. These goals should be a mix of long-range and short-term goals. Even daily goals will help the company achieve a lot more than it would if there were no goals. A company with no goals is adrift in the sea of daily business activities, reacting to the environment rather than making forward movement. When you're reacting, you're not acting proactively. You're not making forward progress when you are reacting; you're simply maintaining your position or making up for lost ground. Your role, as an owner, is not to simply stay afloat but to sail toward your destination and achieve the final goal of business success.

However, you should strive for a balance between moving ahead and staying afloat. You cannot ignore the problems and situations that will inevitably arise. So, you should not create so many goals that they become a burden to you. Setting too many goals will result in overworking yourself and your employees. You do not want this situation either. As Aristotle said, "You should practice moderation in all things."

Focus

The question you are, no doubt, asking now is, "How can I keep this balance and not overdo the creation of goals?" Well, the answer to this is clear. "Look to your mission!" Any plan that you create should be derived from, and should focus on, performing your business' mission. Everything you do in business should be consistent with this mission and should not divert your attention and resources toward activities that are nice to have or exciting to explore, but that do not relate to your area of business.

This advice seems to violate the entrepreneurial spirit because it is advising the entrepreneur to hold back on being creative. That is true. But you must realize that too much of anything can kill a system. I have seen businesses destroy themselves by adding too many activities that don't relate to the mission or by adding too many activities prematurely.

If, for example, you're in the interior design business, you should think twice about adding a house painting function to this business. The activities are too different for one thing. On the other hand, the house paining business could easily eat away some of the resources of the design business that are needed to support the design business. If you, the owner, have personal, financial resources and want to devote these resources to a new project, it is better to start a new business that can sustain itself through the resources you provide it. Don't set up a situation where one business supports another. The chance of having organizational and legal problems is too great.

Another problem you should guard against is expanding your company too fast with functions that *do* support your mission. The problem with this practice is that when the business is growing too fast, you are not strengthening its foundation. Signs of a business that is growing too fast are lack of a defined organizational structure and lack of written procedures. In other words, all of the kinks are not worked out of the business and it is not sufficiently matured. Another sign of a business that's growing too fast is that it hasn't built up the required capital to support the smaller mission before it is being required to support a broader or larger mission. You know this is the case when you're constantly operating on a shoestring—unable to meet payroll, unable to advertise effectively, unable to pay yourself, for example.

So, once again, developing patience is the key to effectively growing your business. Even though the ideas are coming to you fast and furiously, you don't have the luxury of acting on those ideas too quickly. Write them down and save them for a time when you can implement them successfully without destroying other parts of your company.

Key Points

1. Business planning is as simple as identifying a goal and creating steps to reach that goal.
2. Business plans can be simple or complex. A simple plan is more helpful than no plan at all.
3. Plans should be recorded in writing because plans change and if you do not have a means of measuring the change, you cannot analyze it and make effective corrections.
4. Writing clear goals is a key to creating success in your business.
5. Make sure the goals relate to or support your mission. In this way, you will avoid dissipating your energy or losing focus on what is important to do for your company's success.
6. After you have written a set of goals and objectives, you should work consistently toward progress on a daily or weekly basis.

"In preparing for battle I have always found that plans are useless, but planning is indispensable."
—DWIGHT D. EISENHOWER, ARMY GENERAL AND FORMER PRESIDENT

7.

FUND FOR THE LONG HAUL

"Capital is that part of wealth which is devoted to obtaining further wealth."
— ALFRED MARSHALL, ECONOMIST

WHEN we start our businesses, we have high, positive expectations of early success. This statement is true of every entrepreneur. There are innumerable cases of budding entrepreneurs who have idealistic visions of immediate success— within months of startup—who find that the few thousands of dollars they invested didn't take them through the years of struggling growth they inevitably experience. So, they run out of money and resources before the business learns to crawl. This is a major reason why over 85% of new businesses fail within five years of opening their doors.

These positive expectations are natural but they are often unrealistic in most cases. I encourage you to talk with other business owners—struggling and successful—to find out whether their expectations matched the reality of what they experienced. I believe you will find that business success came slower than expected in all cases. If they were overly optimistic, their under-capitalization severely threatened their ability to survive. Insufficient capitalization occurs when you do not have sufficient funds available to pay bills or grow your business.

Of course, there are exceptions. Not every business will experience such financial struggles. I did not experience it with the training and development company I helped create. It was a three-person partnership. We each invested $1000 for administrative and marketing activities. Our secret to success, however, was to start out with a written plan that we wrote together and followed strictly. We acquired contracts based on benefits-laden proposals and received payment up front due to an ironclad guarantee of satisfaction. By this means, we were able to avoid debt and the result was a 45% return on our investment within a few months.

Carefully Estimate Your Needs

Most inexperienced business owners plan to the level of their anticipated needs and fail to add a cushion to their startup capital. While it is good to have positive expectations for your business, you should also plan for the eventuality that things will go wrong. The question, you may have now is, "How much extra should I plan to have over my expected needs?" Well, there is no certain way of knowing but there are rules of thumb you can use to estimate your real needs.

The easiest thing to do is talk to other entrepreneurs in your industry about their experiences. Ask them what they experienced and try to find out why they had the experiences they describe. In other words, put their experiences in context to help you interpret them more accurately.

It is safe to say that, depending on the industry, the size of the business, and the development model that's being used, it will take three to five years for most businesses to become self-sustaining. This estimate is borne out by the Small Business Administration's statistic that most new businesses fail within their first five years.

For every business I have started, I planned on having an operating cushion of funds to last through three lean years. This means that I was prepared to invest in the business with no return for three years and have enough money to live on during the same period. When I needed the cushion, I was happy to have it. When

I didn't need as much, I was even happier. But the most important consideration to me was that I always had enough money to feed the business and nourish it enough to allow it to grow.

Focus On The Marketing Battle

Most businesses fail because they don't have enough capital to survive. This fact cannot be stressed too much. Sometimes the owner does not have sufficient financial reserves to live on and have to give up her dream to get a "real job," or the business does not have enough money to attract clients. In the latter case, the business suffers because of weak or no marketing. No business can survive without adequate marketing in a broad range of forms; advertising, promotions, direct or indirect mail campaigns, TV and radio commercials, infomercials, fliers and brochures, etc.

This thought brings us to a principle that every business owner should learn and act on. That principle is that you cannot grow your business without a marketing strategy. Marketing activities are absolutely necessary to letting the public know, a) that you are selling what they need or want, b) that what you're selling best satisfies the needs or desires they have, and c) that no one else can satisfy their needs or desires as well as you can.

When you fail to inform the public of these three characteristics of your business, you are only "playing at" being a businessperson. You are not seriously in the marketplace to succeed.

The need for the first activity is based on the fact that, if you're in a viable industry, there will be other businesses in that same industry competing with you. Many, if not all of them, are advertising their services or products. You cannot afford to be hidden in the marketplace. You need to let buyers know what you sell.

As for the second activity, the market may know what you sell but may not be aware that a) they have a problem that you can solve with your offering, or b) that your offering actually meets their need. In either case, you need to tell them the benefits of your service or product.

The final activity is necessary to single you out as the one to go to for satisfying their needs. You need to take it a step further, however, and not just set yourself up to be the first source that comes to their mind to satisfy their needs. You should be positioned as the ONLY source they think of as their provider.

Therefore, you must recognize the need for marketing and devote enough money to your marketing budget from the very outset. If you build it, they will NOT come if they don't know about it. Many struggling business owners never learn this lesson and, consequently, their businesses suffer from marketing anemia.

Create And Follow Your Budget

Besides initiating a viable marketing strategy, the second most important financial need to insure that the business has enough money to survive is a current budget. A budget is a simple tool that comprises two parts, a plan and a review. You can get a free budget template and other financial forms at www.AskJerry-TheFixer.com.

The budget is an estimate of how much you anticipate spending on the various elements of your business. This estimate can be based on what you spent in previous years. But if you have no history because you didn't keep records or because you are just starting out, it can be based on assumptions—but not guesses. The difference between assumptions and guesses is that assumptions are based on evidence and guesses are based on nothing tangible.

Where do you get the assumptions if you have no history? You get them from researching what other businesses spent in similar circumstances. You can get this information from talking with business owners in your industry or talking with your professional service providers such as accountants, bookkeepers, bankers or consultants. The point is that the information is out there and you don't have to rely on wild guesses, which are not helpful at all.

What do these budgetary assumptions look like? Well, the most basic assumption you will make is that what has happened in the past (in your business or in typical businesses within your industry) will follow a similar pattern. On top of this assumption, you will assume that changes to this pattern will take place based on past and expected changes in the business environment. For example, if you spent $8,500 to attract 100 new clients, you can expect to spend another $8,500 to attract another 100 clients but with the cost of living rising by 3% over the past year, you can add another 3% rise to the $8500 in the coming year. Now, the budget for attracting 100 new clients should be around $8755. Does this mean that you will definitely attract 100 more clients if you spend $8755? Not necessarily, but it gives you a reasonable target on which to base your expectations.

The review phase of the budget entails recording what you actually spent and received, measuring the difference, then attributing the most likely reasons for the difference. If you don't take this final step of making an analysis and judgment, the budget will do you no good because the mere difference between the expectation and the actual result will not help you plan. You will not know what adjustments to make.

Now that you have a budget, the next issue is, "How should I manage the budget?" The answer to this question is a lot less certain. Let me illustrate this with an example. A former client had been convinced of the need to create a budget because too many of the company's managers were making financial decisions without considering other company needs. Money was being spent without paying attention to the company's goals or priorities.

Well, this owner created his budget and asked to see the budget everyday. The result of such excessive scrutiny was almost just as disastrous as not having a budget because he wanted to react to all discrepancies as soon as they surfaced. When managing the budget, you must take a balanced approach and look for trends, not simply changes. You should only look for these trends over a reasonable period; monthly, quarterly, semi-annually, or annually.

Protect Your Cash Flow

Another very important tool that is available to you to help increase your profitability more quickly is the cash flow statement. This report tells us how much cash is flowing through our business as well as the amount of cash that is quickly available to meet short-term debts. It is not the same as the income (profit and loss) statement. The income statement can tell us whether our company is profitable or not and where each element of the business is operating effectively or not. The cash flow statement, on the other hand, tells us whether we have enough cash on hand at any given time to pay bills or take advantage of growth opportunities that might unexpectedly surface.

Look at the sample income and cash flow statements at www. AskJerry-TheFixer.com. Notice that the financial categories they are focused on are different. The income statement is focused on whether money is coming in (For example, net sales, gross margin, and net income) or leaving (For example, operating, administrative, and personnel expenses) the company and for what reasons. The cash flow statement, on the other hand, is concerned with those elements where transfer of funds are made (For example, cash receipts and disbursements, purchases, borrowing, tax payments) and when they are made (current or long-term), resulting in how much cash you have on hand.

Evaluate Operational Effectiveness

Business owners, who don't have a financial picture of the health of their companies, cannot make quick, effective decisions. Sure, they can make decisions based on guesses—flying by the seats of their pants. But these are not good management decisions. The chances of your making the right decision while flying by the seat of your pants, as opposed to relying on your flight instruments (*Income Statement, Budget, Cash Flow Statement,* and *Balance Sheet*), are no better than 50-50. The chances of consistently making the right decisions are probably a lot worse than that.

This brings us to the objection of so many business owners who talk themselves into incompetence by claiming that they have never been good with numbers, or that it is too complicated for them to learn to read and interpret these tools. You don't have to look far to find someone who had the same attitude just a few years ago. This was my weakness in business, or so I thought. It limited my effectiveness as a manager for many years and limited what I could do for my fledgling company until I decided to talk myself out of this destructive attitude. I finally realized that those who defended their limitations get to keep them. This was my epiphany and I didn't want to commit to my own weakness. As many of you will find when you take this warning to heart, reading and understanding financial statements are very easy to do and will save you time when you look at these tools periodically.

Don't just think you can bypass this management responsibility by asking an employed manager, your bookkeeper, or your accountant to keep an eye on these for you. If you ask someone to do this for you, you should <u>also</u> require that he teach you at the same time. I've seen too many cases of managers who have let someone hijack their businesses because they trusted another person to manage the financials without checking behind this person. You can be assured that no one will have the same commitment to your vision as you have and you can be assured that some people cannot resist the temptation to take advantage of an opportunity, no matter how much of a "friend" you consider the person to be. The worst case I've seen was that of a couple of friends who owned a nightclub in partnership. One was in charge of the front of the house and the other was responsible for the office administration. After several months of struggling, the front manager learned that the partner was taking $25,000 per month out of the company for his own projects.

Because of this and many, similar incidents I've seen in several industries, I cannot stress, strongly enough, the need for the business owner to jealously guard and control the finances of the company. By extension, if the business is a partnership, each partner has this very same responsibility. In the case of a corporation, every director on the company's board has this very same obligation. It is only by actively managing the business' funds that you can have any assurance of reaching profitability as quickly as possible.

Key Points

1. No matter how confident you are in the imminent success of your business, you should plan conservatively. Plan for the worst-case situation.
2. Plan to fund a robust marketing campaign, recognizing that marketing is the key to business growth
3. Employ all marketing tools available, not simply advertising.
4. Create a company-wide budget and budgets for each major activity. Budgets help you plan your needs and allocate your resources effectively.
5. Pay closer attention to cash flow than to your net profit. A business can be profitable and fail because of poor cash flow.

6. Learn to read and interpret all of your financial documents; Income Statement (P&L), Cash Flow Statement, Budget, and Balance Sheet. These are easy to understand and give you a vivid picture of your entire company's operations.

"Never spend your money before you have it."

—THOMAS JEFFERSON, STATESMAN

8.

PROMOTE CREATIVELY

"If people aren't going to talk about your product, then it's not good enough."
—JEFFREY KALMIKOFF, AUTHOR

"If you don't make your product attractive, then people will not talk about it."
—JERRY PRADIER, BUSINESS MENTOR

EVERY business needs to promote its offerings, but not every business needs to buy advertising. Advertising can cost a lot of money. Promotion can cost very little, if done right. Effective, low cost, promotion is generally called "guerilla marketing." It should be the goal of every business owner to market effectively while spending as little as possible on advertising. Since many businesses must advertise, however, we will describe how to make effective use of this form of marketing (advertising) and describe techniques for effective marketing that are sure to save you money (guerilla marketing). The more money you save on marketing, the more funds you have available for other uses that contribute to profitability.

Advertising Principles

Advertising is communicating information about your business, your services, and your products that is purchased from a third party. Advertisements may be communicated in print media; newspapers, magazines and journals, mail, or billboards. It may be communicated electronically on the radio, television, the Internet, or by mobile device. Advertising is non-personal and attempts to make use of design elements to capture the attention of those individuals who are potential clients.

Advertising is the most expensive form of marketing because you are paying a third party to provide services or a venue—a position in the print media or time slots on radio or TV—to make the advertising possible. To get the most desirable services and venues you have to contend with the problem of supply and demand. So, you can expect to pay premium rates for the best exposure and positioning.

Since advertising costs are high, you need to create strategies for making your advertising campaign as effective as possible. Even if you hire an ad designer to do the work, you need to know the principles of effective design to make sure you are getting value for your dollar.

There are several general principles of advertising that independent business owners need to follow but tend to violate. If these principles are followed, they will automatically get a better return on the money they spend on advertising. The following is a list of the most important principles.

1. **Focus On Benefits.** Benefits address the needs and desires of our potential buyer. They answer the WIIFM (What's in it for me?) question. This question is the only issue in the mind of the buyer. However, advertisers tend to focus only on features because features are easier to describe. Consequently, the seller ends up creating ads that do not talk to the buyer and this causes the message to fall flat.

   So, what's the difference between a feature and a benefit? A feature is a characteristic of a thing (service or product) that distinguishes it from similar objects or concepts.

Everything that you can think of has many features; size, color, shape, cost, duration or life span, material composition, thickness, solidity strength, weight, age, guarantee, name, etc. It is easy to describe a product or service by these characteristics (features) and that is where most advertisers limit their messages. However, every feature that is built into a product or service is added for a reason—for a benefit. So, it is not a wild claim to say that every design feature of your product or service has a corresponding benefit.

For example, a Styrofoam (feature) coffee cup has the benefit of keeping the coffee warm (benefit) while preventing burns (benefit). If the cup has a handle (feature), the handle makes it easier to hold or grip (benefit) and limits the possibility of burns (benefit). If it has a logo (feature), the logo helps the seller brand (benefit) the coffee.

2. **Buy In Bulk.** Purchasing advertising one ad at a time is definitely more expensive than purchasing the advertising in bulk or as an advertising campaign or package. You should never place a single ad and expect it to get beneficial results. It takes several viewings of an ad for it to register on the potential buyer's subconscious and to create a desire to buy. So buying one ad and expecting it to perform effectively is simply dreaming.

The other reason for buying in bulk relates to the complexity of ad design. Creating and tweaking ads to draw out their most effective design elements take work. There are many elements in ads that contribute to or take away from the ads' effectiveness, whether they are display ads, TV ads, infomercials, or radio ads. The only way to evaluate these elements is to tweak them in various printings of the ads to determine which get better or poorer responses. You cannot do this by buying single ads and running them once or twice. When buying ads, ask for the medium's rate card. Determine, within your budget, what advertising package you can afford and create a plan to maximize the effectiveness of the group of ads you buy. This brings us to the next principle of advertising.

3. **Track Your Ads.** In order to determine how each variation of your ad is performing, you need to be able to identify which changes generate the biggest responses. The easiest way to find out which ads are working is to ask your buyers where and when they saw your ad. The responses will tell you which variation of the ad they remember. Record their answers in a chart because you will have to compare the results after you test several versions of the ad. You cannot make an accurate comparison and analysis if you simply keep the data in your head and try to remember what people told you. At best, your memory will be hazy.

You might find that buyers do not remember the variation or location of the ad that prompted their response. Therefore, another easy tactic you can use for tracking is to place a different code in each variation of your ad to force the client to accurately report the ad. For example, each version of your ad might direct the reader to ask for a different individual, respond to a different office or suite number, send a response to a specific address code, or bring in a coded coupon. Each of these techniques can be effective in identifying the version of the ad the buyers have seen. Once you have identified the version of the ad that pulls in the most buyers or inquirers, go with that ad for subsequent campaigns.

4. **Use Professional Ad Designers.** Many new entrepreneurs have absolute pride in their businesses or products and want to show it. Consequently, they take full responsibility for presenting their offerings in the marketplace and don't trust others to design their ads. They end up creating their own ads. Sometimes they create their ads to try to save money. This type of thinking is misguided. If you think so highly of your product, service or business, you should want to spend the money to find someone who can present it in its best light. If you don't have the training or talent for ad design, you should not attempt to create an ad for your offering or business. Yet, what we see, especially in newspapers and local magazines, are hundreds of display ads that look the same and are of the same poor quality. None stands out because "homemade ads" tend to repeat the bad design elements of others that have gone before them. It's the classic case of the blind leading the blind. Unknowledgeable owners repeat the mistakes of unknowledgeable owners, resulting in ineffective and costly advertisements.

However, many media firms have excellent ad designers on staff who are willing and able to design effective ads for you at no extra cost. You should ask if they have these resources and take advantage of this highly developed skill, especially if you do not have to hire an independent design firm to create your ads. But, before blindly trusting your ads to these media employees, you should ask for examples of their work and evaluate the work of several designers against each other to choose the one that best meets your needs. For a concise and comprehensive discussion of those design elements, I encourage you to sign up on OnlineBusinessKnowledge.com or go to AskJerry-TheFixer.com for this help.

5. **Focus On the Target Market.** We've explored this principle in an earlier chapter. Don't waste your money or ad copy trying to appeal to everyone because the best you can hope for is to appeal to NO ONE. It sounds counterintuitive but it is a proven fact that if you limit your audience you will be more effective. Not everyone has the same needs or wants as everyone else. The reason you create ads is to appeal directly to the needs and desires of the potential client. The better you can address those specific needs and desires, the better response you will get from the ads. When you have a highly targeted message, you will be able to create a stronger and more compelling case to buy what you're selling.

If you try to speak to everyone in your ad, your message has to be general. The more general it is, the weaker your message will be. The best message you can hope to give to a generalized audience is, "Buy from me because I'm selling X." How compelling is that? You leave your reader wondering, "WIIFM?" If you're not solving specific problems or providing clear benefits to the reader, you will not convince anyone to buy from you. So, as we stated earlier, every ad you create should be peppered with benefits because, "Benefits sell." Those benefits should be directed only at those individuals who need, or can use, them. For a description of how to identify this audience or market, see Chapters 3 and 4.

Guerilla Marketing Strategies

Guerilla marketing is the most effective form of promotion any business can use. It costs very little and can be used on a daily basis in virtually any setting. The following are two major guerilla-marketing tools business owners often fail to use or fail to use effectively.

Networking Tactics: Networking is simply connecting with others for leveraging your ability to sell. The best way to network is to set a goal and meet as many people as possible. Talk to friends, family members and associates about what you do and how you do it. Don't keep it a secret. Be proud of what you do and you will see how much support you will get in return. Many prospective entrepreneurs have the mistaken belief that they should keep their business enterprises to themselves to keep others from stealing their ideas. This thinking is totally antiquated and false because chances are that no one will have an idea that is totally new or different from what has gone before. In fact, if your idea is so new or different, you should be wary and seriously reconsider whether you want to do something that is not proven in the marketplace. Your best bet is to do something that is successful so that you can capitalize on the desires of the marketplace. If you try to sell an idea, product or service that no one has heard of or that no one has expressed a desire to have, your job of educating the market about its benefits is much harder and more expensive. So, your best bet is to find something that is already known and selling well so that you can jump on the marketing bandwagon.

Another effective networking technique is attending meetings and events of clubs and civic or business organizations. However, you should attend with only one goal in mind. The only appropriate goal for attending these gatherings is to collect contact information from each attendee. Your goal should not be to give them your contact information, even though you will share this with them. Collecting contact information is the best tactic you can use for growing your business or getting sales and it is never too early to start doing this. However, be careful that you don't approach this tactic in a way that labels you as a "card swapper."

Instead, you should create a natural reason for an exchange of personal information. With a file of hundreds of potential or actual clients, you will be able to sell to them whenever you have a sales campaign. You will have an arsenal of warm contacts that will listen with more interest to your sales pitches. The most helpful contact information you can get is the email address because it will cost you much less in time and money to contact prospects *via* email than by phone or regular "snail" mail.

For requesting contact information at social or business events, I suggest you prepare an effective and responsive elevator pitch that subtly gets the information you need. For an example of an effective elevator pitch, see www.AskJerry-TheFixer.com.

Promotion Tactics: There are many opportunities for you to subtly promote your business or offerings to the marketplace. Some of these cost no, or very little, money. Some cost nothing but your time. The following are a few options that have very high return on your marketing investment.

1. **Press Releases**–A press release, sometimes called a "business brief," is a short, factual announcement of some development or activity in your business. Virtually all newspapers and business journals print these news reports about businesses without charge. The most important thing you should remember is that these are not ads for your business. They are newsworthy announcements about you and your business. So, do not use them to advertise sales or compare your offerings to the offerings of your competitors. Keep all adjectives out of your press releases and chances are you will avoid writing an ad. You should not hesitate to write a press release about yourself or your company; a promotion of someone within your company, a new acquisition, a training opportunity you are offering or have taken advantage of. Write about any newsworthy

activity or event that could be of interest to readers of the publication.

Since, press releases are published at no charge, there is no guarantee that your release will be printed or that it will be published as written. Plus, you will be competing for space with other business news items. So, you need to submit your releases in a way that will give it a better chance for publication. The following are a few suggestions that work well.

a. Before you consider preparing press releases, establish personal and business relationships with one or more reporters, writers or editors at your target publications. These individuals will be helpful in guiding your releases through the system for getting published. Don't expect, however, to get something for nothing. You should identify a benefit you can provide them in return. This could be a lead on a story, a new advertising candidate, or a promotional opportunity for them. If you belong to a civic organization in common with them, this common membership might provide opportunities for you to offer something in return for their helping you in your promotional activities.

b. Ask for and follow the directions the publications give you for submitting releases. If you do not have this information, follow these guidelines. Most publications prefer to get press releases via email rather than by hard copy. Many prefer you to use a more legible font such as Arial and to create the release with double spacing. Provide all contact information; phone, fax, email, mailing address or business location.

c. Submit a picture of the person or event you are promoting. Pictures make the release more interesting.

Make sure the digital photos are at least 300kb in size. The larger the photo size, the easier it will be for the publication to edit them.

d. Do not submit an item with a short deadline for printing. Expect at least a two-week wait for your release to be published in a daily newspaper.

e. Do not pester your contacts or the editors about when your release will be printed. These individuals may be working on deadlines and do not need, or will not appreciate, the distractions.

f. Before submitting the release, let your contact(s) know that you are doing so and send them a copy.

2. **Sponsorships**–These are opportunities to support— with money or in-kind services—charitable or community projects while attaching the name of your business to this support. You do not have to be a sole sponsor of an event in order to benefit from the promotional activities leading up to and following the events. Offer to co-sponsor at a lower level of sponsorship. Offer a challenge sponsorship to other businesses to leverage and maximize your donation. I once offered a challenge sponsorship to other businesses and received advertising equal to that of the title sponsor. Another time, through shrewd negotiation, I received a prime position on a full-page event ad (opposite the schedule page) for the cost of a half-page ad. Sponsorships can result in a lot of publicity for less cost than display ads in standard publications. Sponsorships also brand your company as a supporter of the community.

3. **Donations to Auctions**–If you are aware of open or silent auctions that are being held in your community, contact the event planners and offer a service or product to be included. They will appreciate your offering and you will benefit by

having low-cost promotional opportunities. Along with your offering, provide your brochures, cards and your own displays that give adequate descriptions of your business. It also helps to volunteer for these events if you cannot attend as a paying guest, to view how your offerings are being displayed. If you are not satisfied with the promotion you get from these, make a request for better positioning or refrain from offering to the ones who do not sufficiently show their appreciation for your products or services. I often donate services to high-profile, high-cost auctions because it helps to have my business name displayed along with much bigger and higher profile companies. Just be judicious about which causes, with which you decide to be associated. Make sure they complement your branding efforts.

4. **Speaking and Writing**–Many people cringe at the thought of writing or speaking. However, both are extremely effective in promoting yourself or your company.

You should try to write for a local newspaper or magazine. If you do this, you should write articles of local interest. Otherwise, you will not get published in local media. Another option is to produce a regular newsletter that contains helpful advice or hints related to your industry or to your client's needs. If you are not a good writer, this should not be a hindrance. You can hire a ghostwriter. Go to Elance.com or Guru.com to hire writers for very reasonable rates. On these sites, you can compare work they have done and prices they charge. Another option is to reprint articles from other newsletters and ezines. To find ezines that are related to your specialty or interest, go to ezine-dir.com, ezinelisting.com, subs.zinester.com, or jogena.com. Just make sure you read and follow the directions for reprinting these and follow the instructions to the letter to avoid copyright infringement. Writing keeps your name in front of the public's eyes on a regular basis and costs little to nothing. Reminding your potential clients that you're here, helps them remember you when they need what you're selling.

Another option you have is to give talks to civic, charitable and community organizations within your market area. Organizations such as Lions, Rotary, and Civitan chapters as well as chamber of commerce groups, some leads groups and networking groups regularly schedule speakers on a variety of topics for the benefit of their members. Just be careful that you do not present a live infomercial about your company. No one wants to be captive to an extended commercial. Make your presentation helpful and informative to the audience. Before the presentation, ask the program director to describe the audience who will be present. Create or tailor a presentation that will help them in some way. I have prepared ten 15- to 20-minute PowerPoint presentations that I regularly present. Using PowerPoint helps provide an outline for the talk and engages more of the audience members' senses. At each presentation, I acquire at least one prospective client who makes an appointment to talk further. Not only does it cost me nothing except time, but I have met many interesting individuals I would not have met otherwise. See OnlineBusinessKnowledge.com for additional suggestions on making such presentations.

If you are creative and remember to think from the potential customer's point of view, your promotional activities will be successful. If you insist on not standing out from the crowd and are content to do what everyone else does to promote their businesses and offerings, you will get no better results than the majority of your competitors. Your results will only be mediocre and not stellar. You might survive in business but if mere survival is not the reason you started your company, why should you settle for it?

Key Points

1. Advertising is a necessity for most businesses. However, it doesn't have to cost an exorbitant amount if you do it correctly by focusing on benefits, buying in bulk, tracking your ads, using professional ad designers, and focusing on a target market.
2. Take advantage of effective guerilla marketing techniques to maximize the promulgation of your message for very little cost.
3. Use networking and promotional techniques to constantly and inexpensively keep your business in the minds of your potential clients.

> *"In the factory we make cosmetics; in the drugstore we sell hope."*
> CHARLES REVSON, COSMETICS INDUSTRY EXECUTIVE

9.

CULTIVATE PARTNERSHIPS

"In the past a leader was a boss.
Today's leaders must be partners with their people...they
no longer can lead solely based on positional power."
—KEN BLANCHARD, BUSINESS AUTHOR

No one is an island, especially business owners. Business owners cannot separate themselves from clients, of course, because without clients, doing business is impossible. Most also must deal with employees, vendors and contractors to run profitable businesses. But there are other groups of people business owners need to rely on if they are to be successful. They are, in a very real, but not legal, sense, "partners." We will discuss the various classifications of partners in some detail because they are very important in leveraging our talents and resources for making bigger profits quickly. Partners can be business associates, advisors and competitors. Again, I'm not limiting members of this category to legal business partnerships. The secret to choosing the right partners for your business is to look for positive-energy generators.

These business resources are helpers, cheerleaders, or reality checkers. Even those who warn us of problems ahead can be positive influences if they can also tell us how to avoid the problems and prevent their recurrence. So, it is important for every business owner to cultivate the right relationships with the right people in each of these categories. This chapter will guide you in selecting the right ones for the job.

Business Associates

Even the most experienced business owners and entrepreneurs need the services of certain specialists to help grow their businesses. Specialists you hire may fall into many categories. We will describe some of these later. But let's start by mentioning the two types of specialists that every business owner needs to hire.

No matter what negative stories or opinions you hear about lawyers and accountants, I hope you realize that there are some business activities that require you to work with them. The danger of making legal or accounting mistakes is too great for you to rely on your own instincts or on the advice of untrained business owners. These professionals comprise two of the most highly specialized and regulated services that help you structure your business correctly. Any profession that requires licensure has to meet specific standards to prevent the untrained from giving faulty advice. So, if you don't have a go-to accountant or business lawyer to help you start your business, you are behind the power curve. You are asking for trouble.

Besides helping structure your company, they can be of great benefit to help navigate your business through the fog or through rough waters. You do not have to consult them frequently. An occasional (annual) check-in will serve your business well.

These two professions are not the only professional business service providers (PBSPs) you may need. They are also not the only two PBSPs whose advice, if good, will help your business thrive and, if bad, will cause you great harm. Other PBSPs may include business consultants, marketers, financial advisors, bankers, bookkeepers, and others.

Every PBSP that works for your business must be selected with care. It is not the case that a bad fit is necessarily incompetent or malicious. As in every field, there are areas of focus and specialization that need to be considered. If you select the wrong

PBSP for your business or for your personality, you're delaying your progress toward becoming profitable. Now let's look at several other PBSPs and explain their roles and value to businesses.

When you select PBSPs (Pronounced, "PIBS") for your company, you should consider these principles.

Your PBSP is your trusted agent and is an important asset that is not part of your business. This person should be a great fit for your business and your personality.

Interview several PBSPs in a given profession before selecting one. Find out their hourly rates and the services for which they charge and do not charge. There is a wide range of rates and wide discretion in all of these areas. You may be able to negotiate lower rates for some or all services. You may get them to provide free oral advice if it takes less than a certain number of minutes or if it is not face-to-face. You may even be able to negotiate a fixed rate per month for an unlimited number of consultations–called "fixed-price agreements." You should have reasonable access to the service provider when you need help and should be able to expect an answer within a reasonable amount of time.

To help you with your selection of PBSPs, your interviews should be focused on getting the following information.

- ✓ How large is the firm?
- ✓ What are the service rates?
- ✓ What is the size of their clientele?
- ✓ For what services do they charge and not charge
- ✓ After how many minutes does the charging clock start?
- ✓ How many years has the firm been in business?
- ✓ What percentage of small to medium to large businesses do they serve?
- ✓ How many years has it been specializing in businesses of your size?
- ✓ How many clients in your industry does it have?

✓ Who, in the firm, will be working on your account?

✓ How comfortable are the professionals in the consulting field?

✓ What is their advisory style?

✓ What is their personal deadline for getting back to clients with answers or acknowledgements of their questions?

✓ Will you have a designated professional handling your account or several firm members?

✓ What is the contact information of some of their clients that are closest to your business or industry? (You want to get references.)

The following are individuals who are available to help your business succeed. You should consider seeking their help and, in some cases, you must seek their help to grow your business.

Attorney – I tell all new business owners to identify an attorney to help with business setup. The biggest benefit of an attorney is to help you decide what type of business entity you should choose to register your business—sole proprietorship, partnership, limited liability company, S-corporation, or C-corporation. These are not the only options you have for registration but they are the most common. Ask the attorney on what basis you should choose a particular business designation (Sole proprietorship, partnership, LLC, S- or C-Corp). You should understand why your business is registered as it is.

As far as the actual registration is concerned, an attorney is not necessary to accomplish this task. You may be able to accomplish the registration yourself on the Internet. You should search the Secretary of State's site within the state you're registering your company. You do not need to register the business in the state where you live. Your attorney should be able to advise you regarding this decision on whether to do it yourself or not.

Attorneys are helpful in reviewing and ensuring the legal

correctness of a variety of documents such as personnel policies and contracts. No such document should be implemented without a legal review, whether you create the document or receive one from someone else. This review can save you a lot of money and time in the end.

Banker – First, remember that your banker is not your business partner. Even though your banker is not your legal partner in any sense, the banker is an important asset and aid to help you manage your financial status. She is an important member of your extended team and you should feel confident in her abilities and feel that you can get good advice from her.

One of the first things you should do when you decide to go into business is to select a bank and open a business checking account. This should be done even before you register your business, especially if you are operating as a sole proprietorship. In some cases, you will have to register your business before you can open a bank account. Getting a bank account should be done so that you separate your startup costs from your personal finances. A bank account legitimizes your business in the eyes of clients and vendors as well.

Having a business bank account will help you keep track of all business costs and help you to know when your business becomes profitable. Since many new owners do not consider startup costs, they make false judgments about profitability. I have seen an owner put hundreds of thousands of dollars into his business during startup and when he started signing contracts, he thought he was now making money. He was claiming that he was making a profit before recouping the startup costs. But he was short by at least $200K from becoming profitable. The business was not yet making a profit even though he was starting to make money. Such faulty judgments can come as a shock when you need to provide accurate figures for seeking a loan, attracting investors, or selling the business

Your bank may come in handy in many ways besides as a repository for your business funds. You can use the help of your banker to get additional funds for a variety of purposes. This help may be in the form of a loan or letter of credit. When first interviewing bankers, do so with an eye to your future needs in this area to find out whether the bank's lending philosophy and practices match your company's character and likely future needs.

Accountant – When it comes to getting your financial house in order, there's no better time to start then when you start your company. Therefore, I advise every new business owner to select and consult the right accountant for the business. There are many services this PBSP can provide that will save time and money as your company grows. Some of these services are; helping to navigate the startup steps, advising on tax and exit planning, advising on establishing your fiscal year, setting up tax reporting, selecting a bookkeeping method (cash or accrual basis), setting up your financial reports, and advising (along with your attorney) on your business structure or changing it when your business requirements change.

As with the attorney, you should ask the accountant on what basis you should select a business designation (Sole proprietorship, partnership, LLC, S- or C-Corp). Don't be surprised if you get different answers from different advisors. They will be using different criteria for making these judgments and you must analyze and determine which criteria are most appropriate for your situation.

Bookkeeper – Once your financial structure is established, you will have the frequent tasks of updating your records, paying employees and paying taxes. The role of the bookkeeper is to record the daily financial transactions. A bookkeeper keeps records of what is bought, sold, owed, and owned; what money comes in, what goes out, and what is left in the business. An accountant is not necessary to accomplish this work. Most business owners have businesses that are too complex for them to do the work themselves. They hire bookkeepers to perform these tasks. Many independent businesses should contract with independent bookkeepers rather than hire one to work fulltime.

Business Advisor – Many entrepreneurs do not have the staff resources they need to make the wide range of decisions an owner needs to make to help the business succeed. Often, they don't have the training or the experience in marketing, finance, sales, planning, human resources management, policy development or many of the other management and leadership skills they are called upon to carry out. Fortunately, there are experienced executives who provide advice to the independent business owner in a variety of these skills.

These advisors might call themselves coaches or mentors. They might have a narrow range of expertise in one or more specialties but some may be generalists and can help with almost all business management skills. For an example of this general advisory service, see www.probusdev.net.

In my estimation, generalists are more helpful because they can provide you the benefit of analyzing all facets of your company and providing advice that bridges many functions within your company. So, when selecting a business advisor, consider selecting someone who has a wide range of training and experience in running businesses as owners and proven decision makers.

Note that I do not include consultants in this category because consultants are typically hired to analyze a discrete problem and recommend fixes. Coaches and mentors, on the other hand, work hand-in-hand with the owner to solve general management problems. I consider coaches and mentors as one in the same because there is no appreciable difference in their roles. So, I will refer to both as "mentors." Mentors are not substitutes for the owner or manager of the company. They advise the decision maker on actions to take and strategies to adopt but the owner makes the final decisions. A mentor who makes the decisions for the owner is overstepping his limits of authority.

As a business owner, you should be aware that you do not give up your responsibility for running the company, even with the help of a mentor. So, don't expect the mentor to do your work for you. The mentor performs the roles of guide and teacher to the owner. The owner's success or failure in improving operations is a shared responsibility to the extent that the mentor should give accurate advice. But the owner has the responsibility of following through and to the extent he doesn't, he shares responsibility for lack of success.

Executive Coach – The function of an executive coach is different from that of the business mentor, who coaches on how to solve business management problems. The executive coach is a personal mentor who helps the owner focus on personal priorities and helps motivate the owner to achieve personal goals. The following are good examples of how an executive coach can help.

I previously mentored a very successful business that was almost running on autopilot. The owner had established systems and a structure that proved successful over the years. Yet, he recognized that he had a problem that was beginning to affect his ability to react to a changing market. His problem was that he had no inner motivation or strategy for achieving his personal goals and this was evident in the many plans for growing his business that never materialized. So, he asked for personal coaching and I began by helping him identify all of the desires he wanted to satisfy. By doing this, we prioritized these from easiest to hardest to accomplish and started working on the easily achievable goals first. We created a strategy for breaking these down into small steps with deadlines. In this way, we quickly achieved small successes and he began to feel good about these while learning a strategy for accomplishing any goal. In the end, he was on a path that was self-propelling. He was able to apply this methodology, along with creating accountability, to his business goals as well.

Another owner I coached was unable to transition from being a technician to a manager. He continually engaged in negative talk about how he wasn't a manager and how he never understood numbers. Much of my work with him was to change these attitudes by teaching him the skills he thought he lacked, directing him to training that could fill in the knowledge gaps I had no training in, and providing him with opportunities to display his hidden skills by walking him through the processes of making decisions that he felt incompetent to make. This is the benefit of working with an executive coach. You learn personal habits that can be applied across the board to all areas of your life.

I have coached dozens of executives who were in the process of changing careers and going into business for themselves. In addition to helping them adjust emotionally and mentally to the career changes, I helped them to establish goals and deadlines and identified strategies for holding themselves accountable to their deadlines. When self-doubt or confusion surfaced, I guided them through the process of finding out why these thoughts and feelings were causing them to stagnate and miss their goals.

Webmaster – It is becoming increasingly obvious to independent business owners that they need a presence on the Internet. Whether you sell online or not, potential clients tend to look for a web site these days to get more information about companies. A web site, today, almost legitimizes a company in the eyes of the consumer despite the presence of other organizations such as the Better Business Bureau that are designed to do just that. It is just easier to go to a company's web site to get questions answered rather than pick up a phone and get transferred from one department to another for the same information.

Please note that web site creators are not certified or accredited and many go into business with only the rudimentary, technical knowledge to create web sites. They probably do not have training in sales, marketing or artistic design. So, you must be very careful in choosing a web designer and a Webmaster, if these have different roles in your company.

The following are some principles you should consider implementing in the design of your site.

- ✓ Your site is as much a promotional and marketing tool as a display ad in a publication. The design should be as carefully constructed to sell your business or products effectively as any display ad. It should coordinate with other elements of your branding.
- ✓ Unless you have a business in entertainment (movies or music industry), forget the use of Flash and other "flashy" novelty elements. Make it easy and quick for people to go to the information they need on a business site. Flash pages are useless for sales or marketing of your company. Moreover, web spiders do not read their content. So, flash content inhibits establishing your position on search engines.
- ✓ Make sure you pepper your site with capture boxes. One of the most important moves you can make from the very start of your business career is to make as many contacts as you can and get contact information about everyone you encounter. (See Chapter 8) This is called networking. The most important aspect of networking is getting the contact information so that you can communicate with your contacts later. You can use this information to effectively and cheaply advertise your offerings or promote

your company. Capture boxes force your web site visitors to "sign in."

✓ Maintain control of your site by including, in your contract with the developer, the requirement to provide you with all coding and passwords. Make sure the contract specifies that you are the owner of the site and that the developer is being paid to develop the site for you. Seek your attorney's advice on this contract.

Personal Associates

Many businesses should not have a board of directors. Only corporations should and must have a board, by law. A board of directors is a group of individuals elected by stockholders to establish corporate management policies and make decisions to protect the interests of the stockholders. The directors have legal and fiduciary responsibilities to the shareholders. Therefore, it is not appropriate for other business entities such as partnerships or LLCs to have a board.

While not every business needs or should have a board of directors, every business needs a panel of advisors. To be more precise, the owner or top manager of every company needs a group of people who help by sharing experiences, giving trusted, objective advice, and off of whom he can bounce ideas. This panel is an informal, but important tool for any manager to have as an aid in decision making.

This group of informal advisors has no legal standing in the company and no legal fiduciary responsibilities. No company has a legal obligation to have a panel of advisors but every business owner has a moral obligation to herself to gather a trusted team on which to rely for help in running the business.

Two of the most common questions I get about the panel of advisors are, "Who should be in this group?" and "How large should it be?" The answer to the first is, the panel may be composed of other business owners, family members, friends, selected clients, or personal heroes. You should consider and ask anyone whose opinion you trust and with whom you can be open about your business issues. If these individuals are your friends, that's a good start because you will be starting with people you trust to some extent.

The answer to the second question is that they can be any number you want them to be. That number can change at any time; depending on how much help you need at any given time. You may meet with your advisors at any time or as frequently as you want and there is no need to convene a meeting of your advisors at any time. I have a number of advisors who live across the country. I talk with them periodically and I only meet regularly with the handful of advisors who live nearby. I compensate those with whom I meet regularly by buying them lunch or coffee. To some, I give free promotional opportunities by featuring them on my TV show as business experts in their peculiar fields. Finally, I compensate others by giving them advice and encouragement in return. With the latter, the relationship is mutually beneficial.

One of the biggest problems business owners face within their companies is the danger of being surrounded by people who will tell them what they want to hear. Therefore, they don't have honest brokers that care enough to call them on their bad ideas or actions. So, they never learn until after their mistakes are made. Don't place yourself in this dangerous position. Be open to advice, welcome criticism, and embrace honesty to give yourself a better chance of making decisions that will net you positive return rather than losses from poor decisions.

Business Competitors

If you are a student of big business in the US, you know that CEOs of public corporations and large, private companies tend to associate together, even if they are in the same industries. You will also notice that top executives move around among the same size or types of companies. It is common for large companies to hire the superstars from their competitors or other companies of similar size.

When this happens, friendships that these executives had previously do not suddenly end. They continue to socialize outside of business, join the same social and business clubs, and network with each other by phone or email. Naturally, when this happens, they share common and similar problems and experiences and build social-business bonds that help them remain at the top of their games.

There is no reason why owners of small businesses cannot or should not do the same. Many successful business owners do this. What better person to share your concerns and issues with than someone who is facing or has faced similar issues? Naturally, you do not want to divulge proprietary information about your company or processes with a potential competitor. Therefore, you must be careful of guarding this information that could end up hurting your business.

Approaching competitors to work together for mutual benefit is a business tactic that too few owners employ outside of Internet marketing. If done correctly, it can result in greater benefit for all who cooperate. To explain the logic behind this concept, we need to go to the analogy of marketing as a battle.

This is true, each business is fighting for market share and since market share is limited, each business must look at marketing as a battle to gain as much ground as possible. However, this need not be a win-lose battle. Depending on how you view your market and industry, it can be win-win. Here's a real-life example.

When I was a partner in a previous business, our company had a well-defined market territory of five states in which to sell our services. This company was wildly successful and was profitable after three months of starting. Still the three partners wanted to increase its market share and grow the business. Meanwhile, we noticed that at many of the venues where we provided our services, a direct competitor was also providing services. We knew that this competitor had been in business for many years and was very successful with a company that was much larger than ours. My apparently naïve idea was to approach the CEO of this company to ask him for help in growing our company—to find out tricks of the trade that would make us more successful faster. Against the ridicule and doubt of my partners, I asked for an appointment with this CEO for this very purpose. I was surprised, again, at how quickly he agreed to meet with us in his office in Atlanta for an entire afternoon. He was very open with us and it proved to be a very enlightening meeting. Toward the end of the meeting, even I was surprised when we came to the realization that the market was bigger than what both of our businesses could handle.

In the end, we left with an agreement to work together to share the available work. Since we were in different states, we could benefit our potential clients and ourselves by contracting with each other on jobs that were closer to our respective locations.

Even today, I work with direct competitors in my geographic area by providing them with speaking opportunities and by introducing them to potential clients whose particular needs more closely fit my competition's strengths. I've gotten referrals from competitors to work with clients they could not help and I've given referrals to competitors.

The secrets to making such cooperation work are very simple. First, realize that, in the marketing battle, you are not necessarily competing against other businesses. You're competing against yourself—against your own limitations. Until you become a marketing superstar with a commanding lead in your industry worldwide, you will always be competing against yourself to get better and operate more efficiently at every stage of growth. Second, you need to realize that approaching competitors who are not successful is futile. Struggling businesses will not be disposed toward cooperating because they are operating from the position of loss, making doing business for them a win-lose activity. They are more focused on survival than growth. So, I recommend that you only approach your successful competitors to explore ways in which you might help each other grow. There is strength in numbers and if each has a strong unique selling proposition (USP), each will be a winner.

Boards Of Directors

This group is an integral part of the organization as opposed to the groups and individuals who are mentioned above. The Board of Directors (BoD) is a body of appointed persons who oversee the activities of the company on behalf of the owners (shareholders). A BoD is not appropriate for every kind of business. However, if a business is registered as a corporation, it must have a BoD to oversee executives' decisions and make policy that protects the interests of the shareholders. The responsibilities of the BoD are outlined in the company's bylaws.

Since many businesses register as corporations, it is helpful to discuss the role of the board and point out some considerations that owners need to be aware of to maximize the company's profitability. Misconceptions about the role of the BoD can actually hamper the profitability of the business.

Typical roles of boards include:

✓ Establishing policies and goals;

✓ Appointing, evaluating and supporting the chief executive;

✓ Providing adequate financial resources;

✓ Approving budgets; and,

✓ Answering to the shareholders.

Typically, when young organizations register as corporations, the board is selected by the owner(s) who identify partners and family members to fill these roles. This is only a temporary selection and should be formalized as early as practicable. When filling out or formalizing your board, you should keep the following in mind.

Select members who have some experience in running a business or who have some specialized expertise in business that can benefit your company. Assess your weaknesses and counter them with experts who can fill the gaps.

Select members whom you trust and who are not motivated to take over your business. A BoD can, and has a duty to, remove the chief executive if it believes the executive is ineffective.

Create a BoD composed of an odd number of members, especially if the board is small. Board members, like business partners can disagree and get into power struggles with each other. Just as with partnerships, if there is no deciding vote to break a tie, problems can persist and grow beyond the ability of the business to withstand.

If your company is a for-profit business, you should budget to compensate your board members for the valuable work they perform for your company.

These considerations are necessary for owners to make when creating BoDs for their growing companies. By taking these actions, astute owners will avoid the common problems that restrict fast or steady growth.

These suggestions are, by no means, all one needs to know

about the roles, responsibilities and organization of BoDs. A full description of a board is beyond the scope of this book. So, www. AskJerry-TheFixer.com has resources and a guide for selecting a board.

Key Points

1. No one can effectively run a business on his or her own. Everyone needs advisors.
2. Some advisors should be professional business service providers (PBSPs).
3. The PBSPs may be bankers, accountants, bookkeepers, web masters, mentors, etc. These professionals are paid for their technical expertise.
4. Another group of valuable advisors are your personal associates and friends. Every business owner should identify a group of these people to act as informal advisors to the business. This group is called a panel of advisors and every business should have a panel.
5. The panel of advisors is NOT the same as a board of directors (BoD).
6. The BoD is a legal entity that is required of corporations. This is a formal governing body of the corporation and its primary duty is to protect the shareholders of the business.

> *"If you can run the company a bit more collaboratively,*
> *you get a better result, because you have more...*
> *checking and balancing going on."*
> —LARRY PAGE, GOOGLE COFOUNDER

10

HIRE THE HUNGRY, NOT THE EXPERIENCED

"Enthusiasm is the mother of effort, and without it nothing great was ever achieved."
—RALPH WALDO EMERSON

Some of the most important partners you will have, as your business grows, are your employees. Hiring people who are not suited to your company can quickly deplete money, time, and opportunities for profit from your business. The costs of hiring, training, motivating and compensating employees is one of the biggest your company will experience. If your goal is to create a growing business, you will have to hire employees to help it grow. You only have limited time and ability to perform all of the necessary functions most thriving businesses accomplish. So, if you feel that you do not want the headache of training, supervising and motivating employees, you will eventually realize that you will have to artificially limit the growth of the business without the help employees can provide.

The question business owners must answer first is, "When should we hire someone to help in the business?" The easy answer is to hire when the work grows to be too much to do it alone. But when we make the decision based on this criterion, it is already too late.

We need to plan ahead if we want to remain in charge of our

business rather than remain at the mercy of it. We need to hire employees **before** we absolutely need them in order to make this decision at the right time and in the right way.

Decide To Hire Based On Measurements

We should not make the decision to hire employees based on not having time to devote to the business and our personal lives. We should anticipate this decision based on objective, growth criteria. You should plan your need for growth in your business plan. (See Chapter 6)

Before you can hire, you must recruit. This is an important and complex task apart from the selection. You will have two decisions to make during the recruitment process. The first is to identify what skills you will need. The second is to determine whether an applicant has those skills or the personal qualities that can acquire those skills quickly.

The skills need to be determined at the very start of the business. They should be identified in the business plan to avoid making decisions based on emotions alone. When our decisions are based primarily on emotions, we're simply reacting to the environment. But when they are based on rational choices, they are more proactive and better thought out. We should use rationality as a standard on which to make most of our business decisions.

Therefore, we should decide, early on, to increase our staff based on how we expect our business to grow. These decisions can be made based on the amount of sales increase we achieve, the number of new clients we acquire, the need to open new branches, and many other objective criteria that are measurable and observable. And based on the industry, type of business, and the type of growth we experience, we need to identify those functions and positions that need to be added. The positions might be administrative, technical, or managerial functions.

For example, Let's assume you have a medical practice. You might judge that when your sales reach a total of $13K per month, you will need one clerk to handle the traffic. In this case, you track your sales on a weekly or monthly basis and judge when you will need to hire two or three additional sales clerks. If you want to reach a sales target of $250K per year, you judge that you will need to have two clerks working for you, each handling a business load of $125K per year. Let's say you want to open another medical office approximately 30 miles from your home office. After evaluating the capacity of your current practice, you estimate that you will be able to support a new office if you had 90 additional patients to add to your current 115 patients at the home office. You will base these judgments on objective data and assumptions about costs to run an additional office, personnel costs, projected population growth and the expected retirement of a colleague who serves the area in which you want to expand. Even though your projections and estimates are not based on certainty, these calculations are better than wild guesses or better than finding yourself trapped by a business that has grown unexpectedly fast to the point where you are losing control.

Having a fast growing company is not necessarily as beneficial as you might think. If the business is growing too fast, it may be speeding along the road to early collapse if you're not able to serve your clients effectively. I took on a position with a fast growing company that was about to implode because it was growing too fast for the executives to react. Service was deteriorating and money was being wasted on overtime pay to keep up with the service needs. This business had been wildly successful but its success was destroying it. Upon my starting to work with the business, it had 250 employees and an organizational structure that was developed in reaction to problems that developed over time. The structure that had developed was unable to support a business of its current size. The first thing the owner and I did was to rewrite the business plan. Then we began to restructure the company by identifying appropriate positions and a better organizational structure. In the end, we learned that we could take better care of the clients with fewer employees. We made a commitment not to fire anyone. We would wait for employees to retire or find other career paths to follow. So, through attrition, we were able to resize the company, over time, while steadily increasing the quality of our service. Eventually, everything worked out, preventing the owner from selling off parts of the business or closing the operation altogether.

Whom To Hire

One of the most important questions an owner should answer is what types of people to hire for the various functions. My answer, after over 25 years of experience is simple; hire the hungry. When it comes to selecting among a variety of candidates, one should hire the applicant with the best attitude toward, and reasons for wanting, the job. Hire someone who needs the work and will do what is necessary to prove his worth. You do not necessarily want the person who is the superstar in past jobs for several reasons. This person may be living only on reputation of accomplishments and not on what they can contribute now. She may have the highest of educational level and experience but might be the know-it-all, above receiving direction or training. She might end up being the problem child who refuses to work according to your standards. She might think she is bringing a certain amount of prestige to your business and, that you need her more than she needs you.

So, your best bet, if you don't need someone with required educational or license certifications, is to hire someone you can train. Sometimes the less experienced is the more desirable. The problem you have, however, is knowing how to make this decision. We will cover this in the next section.

How To Hire

The hiring process starts well before you have a need to bring on employees. It starts during the planning process when you create a structure for your organization. The first step is to describe the ideal skills for each position you anticipate needing. This is the best approach because it is always better to describe the functions of an organization without regard to personalities. Many businesses suffer from placing the wrong person into positions, then structuring those positions so that the wrong person will be able to accomplish the tasks. This is the opposite of how successful businesses work. You should hire persons who are the best fit for the position, not the other way around. When you tailor the position to the person, chances are that you will end up with a business that is misaligned or missing crucial functions. This is, generally, the problem I encounter among my clients. The problem stems from not creating a business plan upon starting the business. A good business plan will identify what the company should look like at each phase of growth.

The best technique for creating position descriptions is to identify all the tasks associated with a particular function. Whenever you identify a task or role, you should always identify how well you want it performed. Otherwise, you leave it open to interpretation and argument whether the task was performed correctly or not. For an example of a good position description, see www.AskJerry-TheFixer.com. Notice that it describes all of the tasks that the position's incumbent is expected to perform as well as the standard of performance expected. For example, a **task** might be to, "route correspondence," and the **standard** is, "to the correct recipient."

In the beginning, while the company has few personnel resources, it might be necessary for each staff member to perform multiple functions. So, you may need to assign several positions to a single person. For example, at XYZ Construction, Mary, the owner, would take on the functions of general manager, warehouse supervisor, bookkeeper and outside sales executive, and John, the administrative assistant, would have the additional responsibilities of stockroom clerk and dispatcher. This would leave the technicians to concentrate on providing service to the clients. As the company grows and Mary hires additional employees, she would make sure that the current employees with multiple positions shed the additional roles and concentrate only on their primary roles. So, John would be relieved of warehouse or supply duties and focus more on office administration. This is how position descriptions can help the business grow organically and systematically, maintaining a cohesive organizational structure.

Once you describe the positions that define the structure of the business, the next task is to fill the positions. This is another stage where few business owners get it right and end up delaying the profitability of their companies. They fail to identify the personal traits applicants need in order to perform the jobs satisfactorily and, consequently, they hire people based on the applicants' claims of experience and competence.

What owners should do, however, is describe the personal and professional traits they need for each position. Ideally, these are already part of the position descriptions. After this is done, they should create an interview process to help select the best candidates. A tool that I find very helpful is a set of interview questions that helps to ascertain the personality of the applicant. Each position should have its own set of questions specific to the requirements of the job. Some questions may be factual to give you an idea of how well the applicant knows the job responsibilities. Other questions should be opinion and personal questions to give you an idea of the personality of the applicant. A sample set of questions for interviewing a stock clerk is at www.

AskJerry-TheFixer.com.

It is important to have a set of interview questions tailored to each position. It is also important for you to ask the same questions of all the applicants for a given position and rate their responses against the same criteria. Make sure you also have one or more other managers or supervisors use this very same questionnaire and scale to rate the applicants and compare notes after the interviews. Those with the best scores are selected for the position on a trial basis. This process works exceptionally well. Yet, there are important elements of this process to keep in mind if it is to work effectively.

1. Create the questions for each position **before** the interview and **distribute** these questions to the interviewers so that they will be familiar with the questions and know why the questions are being asked. You want some consistency in judgment, so you should compare the ratings and notes of each interviewer to establish this consistency.

2. How you ask the questions is as important as the questions you ask. You should display a friendly, professional demeanor. Don't be overly friendly, encouraging, discouraging, or joking. These types of behaviors during an interview may end in claims that you discriminated, were unfair, asked illegal questions, or made commitments to applicants. The interviewers should not play "good cop-bad cop." Moreover, interviewers should listen attentively and drill deeply into the answers the applicants give in order to get information that is more useful.

3. Do not vary the questions among the applicants for a given position. Ask each applicant the same questions and use the same interviewers for every applicant. The process has to be fair to everyone. Using this process lessens the risk that your selection process will appear unfair.

4. Don't have only one person make the hiring decision. The more interviewers you have, the better judgments the group will make. One of the interviewers should be the direct supervisor of the applicant because the supervisor will be working closest to the selectee. If the supervisor has the responsibility of developing optimal performance, the supervisor should have the authority to provide input into the choice of personnel.

5. Keep the interview results and applications for at least a year in a special file in case someone challenges the fairness of your process.

With a solid plan and a coherent system, you can make the hiring process less painful and more productive. I encourage you to go to AskJerry-TheFixer.com for more detail and help on the hiring process.

Maintaining Standards

The hiring process is only one element of the personnel process. Having position descriptions is just one tool available for setting standards. You will need other tools to help you establish and maintain peak performance.

Some of the biggest costs a business will incur are personnel costs. Attracting, selecting, training, motivating and compensating employees are major cost elements of doing business. So, you should want to lead and supervise your employees as efficiently as possible. You must, therefore, expect and get top performance for your personnel investment or you will be throwing money down the drain. Every supervisor must aspire to be a leader because leadership encourages your employees to follow you and work to achieve your vision. For a concise description of the practices and traits of a business leader, I encourage you to read, *Lead, Don't*

Manage Your People, by Jim Black. It gives tangible examples of how business people should lead.

Other motivational and teambuilding tools are available to managers to help identify and encourage the standard of work that will help your business grow and prosper. These are divided into reward systems and corrective systems. The reward systems support and encourage desirable behavior and the corrective systems attempt to change undesirable behavior. In this book, we will provide enough detail to give you an idea of the range of actions at your disposal. For a much greater description of these methods, you should go to www.AskJerry-TheFixer.com. But for now, let's mention some of the motivational tools in each category.

Motivational Tools

The most obvious motivational tools managers and supervisors consider are money, to encourage desirable behavior and punishment, to discourage undesirable behavior. However, many studies have shown that money and punishment are some of the least effective motivators in the workplace. Other motivators can be as effective or more effective. For example, training and setting clear expectations are often more effective as motivational tools in response to desirable and undesirable behavior. Note how the US Marine Corps uses pride and tradition to motivate its members to perform some of the toughest duties among all military services. I proved this principle on several occasions as a supervisor in private companies. The most notable is when I managed a security service that had been experiencing a turnover rate of over 75% per year. After implementing several no-cost and low-cost initiatives, we reduced the turnover to less than 5% per year. By instituting a recognition program, a supervisory ride-along program, emphasizing uniform standards, and making other changes, we increased retention.

In addition to the reduced turnover, we saw additional benefits of fewer errors being made by employees and an increase in clients over 18 months. These improvements took effect during a period when we curtailed the automatic raises in favor of lower raises given based on merit.

The following is a list of a few tools you might consider using to motivate your employees to perform more productively. The first ten focus on encouraging or rewarding desired behavior and the last three, on correcting substandard behavior. This is not an exhaustive list. With a bit of creative thinking, you can add to this list of suggestions.

1. Supply your staff with distinctive uniforms or items such as badges, smocks, or caps to be worn while at work.
2. Institute supervisory observations or shadowing to observe the employees' performance. Be sure to comment on or reward admirable performance.
3. Establish an educational or training subsidy for upgrading job-related knowledge.
4. Initiate an employee of the month, quarter or year program to recognize outstanding performers. Be sure to promulgate the criteria for the award.
5. Provide transportation or create a ride-sharing program for employees who live at a distance.
6. Upgrade the employees' workspace, taking the employees' suggestions into consideration.
7. Create a suggestion program. Tie the program into a reward program for suggestions that save or make the company money or improve productivity.
8. Organize employees to volunteer for community service projects.
9. Provide company wide cross-training opportunities.

10. Set high standards and require everyone in the company or division to meet them.
11. Provide in-house training for groups and individuals to upgrade performance.
12. Conduct verbal and written counseling sessions.
13. Express displeasure to include, in order of escalating severity, admonitions, warnings, suspension, and reassignment.

The most effective means of implementing these practices is by creating a performance enhancement and improvement policy and following that policy religiously. By means of such a policy, you will diminish the risk of appearing unfair.

In addition to displaying the leadership qualities that encourage your employees to accept and work for your vision, it is necessary to establish systems that help your organization operate efficiently. Written policies, procedures, checklists and continuity folders will go a long way in helping employees work more effectively and efficiently. By having written procedures, you will avoid the cycle of having to reinvent the wheel every time your company experiences organizational changes. So, in addition to choosing the right person for the position, you have an equal obligation to provide the employee with the tools to perform to their highest ability.

Key Points

1. Hiring the right employees is a key element of business success.
2. The right person for the job is often the one with the best attitude, not the one with the most experience or training.
3. The key to hiring the right person is developing the criteria for the job and matching the person to the position.
4. The hiring process should be predefined and followed

meticulously to give you the best chance of selecting the right person.

5. Your selection is just the first step in finding the right person for the position. All of your employees must be supported with a full range of personal and professional development tools to sustain and improve performance.

6. A business that does not constantly provide opportunities for developing optimal performance will not thrive and experience sustained profitability.

"What counts is not necessarily the size of the dog in the fight - it's the size of the fight in the dog."

—DWIGHT EISENHOWER, ARMY GENERAL AND FORMER PRESIDENT

AFTERWORD

I HAVE known Jerry Pradier for over 30 years and can attest to his business acumen, much of which is included in the preceding pages. His experiences in starting businesses, coaching business leaders, and lecturing to a vast audience of business associates are included in this book. In his book *Financial Success: Ten Shortcuts to a Profitable Business*, Jerry outlines ten shortcuts that will help the entrepreneur, the established business leader and anyone who strives to become a success in business. Beginning with the habits of a business leader, Jerry writes about the need for every successful leader to possess Patience, Persistence and other qualities to make their businesses buzz. I was duly impressed with the thoroughness he displays while writing about the ten shortcuts. He keeps the topics concise and gets to the significant part without losing those ideas that will truly help anyone reading the book.

His coverage of expectations and desires, followed by niche marketing and branding are especially enlightening. Any reader will find the areas compelling and spot on. The author treats the more mundane, but critically important, areas of planning, funding and promoting the business with rigor and in an interesting way. Jerry's positive experiences in these areas clearly come through and the reader will gain an added appreciation for the importance of getting planning, funding, and promoting right.

Chapters 9 and 10, partnering and hiring, respectively, are

particularly strong chapters in the book Jerry adeptly points out the need to treat a myriad of associates as partners in order to make your business successful. He completes his writing with, perhaps, one of the most important ingredients to a successful business. Whether your business is small or large, getting the right person in the job has been, and will always be, critical for a profitable business. The author writes about how attitudes matter—those of the leader and the employee.

If you are operating a business, or if you intend to open a business, this book is necessary for you. If you are having difficulty in your business, or planning for change, you need to read this book. This book should be on the desktop of every entrepreneur and businessperson. It's that good! The book is full of practical, understandable, pertinent advice gleaned from previous business experience. I have often held the belief that if I want to do something I have not done before, the best person to ask about it is someone who has done it successfully. Jerry Pradier is that guy. Read the book. Put all of it into practice. You WILL be successful!

Jim Black, President & CEO
Applied Leadership Services, LLC

GLOSSARY

Advertising: Attempting to influence the buying behavior of your customers or clients by providing a persuasive, informative or descriptive selling message about your products or services; the impersonal communication of information, usually paid for and usually persuasive in nature, about products, services by identified sponsors through the various media.

Attitude: This is a person's state of mind or feeling about a particular thing. In marketing, one's attitude is important to determine a person's needs or desires at any given time.

Brand: A distinguishing mark; name term, sign, symbol, design or combination used to identify the products of a company to differentiate it from competitors; a name consisting of words or letters

Branding: The process of defining a concept that will stay in the minds of your prospects; designing the character of your business that distinguishes it from other products, services, or concepts so that it can be easily communicated and marketed; creating a personalized identity for your company.

Capture Box: A small form on a web site that requests identification information from the viewer before authorizing access to additional information or benefits on the site. Typical capture boxes will ask for a name and an email address.

Continuity Folder: A book or folder containing checklists of procedures for performing various tasks within the company. Every position and every function should have a continuity checklist to save you time and money on training. It can be an effective means of ensuring new employees perform functions correctly.

Debt Financing: The acquisition and use of borrowed funds for the purpose of financing a business. In return for lending the money, the lenders become creditors and receive a promise to be repaid principal and interest on the debt.

Demographics: The physical characteristics of a population such as age, sex, marital status, family size, education, geographic location, and occupation.

EIN: See Employer Identification Number below.

Emerging Business: A startup business or a business in the early stages of its development. This period of emergence can last three to five years and is the most critical period that will determine whether the business will succeed or not.

Employer Identification Number (EIN): This is a nine-digit number used by the IRS to identify a business entity. In general, employer I.D. numbers are needed if a business has employees, has a qualified retirement plan or operates as a corporation or partnership. This is also known as a Federal Tax Identification Number or Federal Employer Identification Number (FEIN). *http://www.irs.gov/businesses/small/article/0,,id=98350,00.html.*

Equity Financing: The acquisition and use of funds by offering ownership in return. Businesses do this by issuing and selling shares of common or preferred stock or taking on a partner in a partnership.

Ezine: This is a recurring publication that is distributed by email or posted on a website.

Fiduciary: Describes the legal requirement to act in the best interest and trust of another. This person has the legal authorization to hold and manage assets in trust for the benefit of another person.

Guerilla Marketing: Low-cost or no-cost advertising or promotions that have high return in terms of generating sales or producing consumer awareness of your company or offerings.

Independent Business: A business that is not publicly owned. It may be a sole proprietorship, a partnership or a corporation. The owner(s) or a managing director may run it.

Incentive: A motivational influence. This is a reward or award that motivates or pushes one to act or perform correctly. The incentive can be different from the justification one gives because the incentive is emotional in nature and the justification is based on reason.

Justification: An explanation, reason or excuse for performing an action or holding a belief.

Leads Groups: These are groups of individuals that get together on a regular basis to share referrals. Unlike networking groups, leads groups restrict the number of people from each category to one representative. That means you will only have one consultant, one accountant, for example. Examples of Leads groups include BNI and LeTip.

Letter of Credit: A letter issued by a bank authorizing the person named to draw money up to a specified amount from the bank, provided the conditions that the letter identifies are met. A document issued by a bank, indicating that the bank will make payments under specific circumstances.

Lifestyles: This is a person's or group's way of living that is dictated by attitudes, values, preferences, opinions, spending habits, or desires. Identifying a lifestyle for a particular person or group tells the business owner what would most likely benefit the target market.

Loan: A given sum of money a borrower may receive from a lender to pay for a purchase. This amount is generally paid back under specific conditions with interest.

Market: The group of people who have a need or desire for your product or service.

Marketplace: The venue for conducting business or making sales; A physical or conceptual area where sales are conducted; The world of commerce; an Internet site where sales are conducted.

Market Segmentation: Focusing on sub segments or niches with distinctive traits that may seek a special combination of benefits.

Networking: The activity of meeting people and telling them about your business to generate interest. It is a form of promotion to create awareness, attract support, of identify potential clients.

Networking Groups: These are groups of individuals who regularly get together to share referrals. Unlike leads groups, networking groups have individuals from many different areas, but do not restrict the number of people from one category. You may have two or more consultants or bankers in a group. There is no exclusivity.

Niche: A special group that is defined by similar needs, desires, or interests.

Niche Market: A narrowly defined group of potential customers. The group of people who have a special need, desire, or interest they want to have satisfied.

Niche Marketing: Addressing a need for a product or service that is not being addressed by mainstream providers.

Offerings: The services or products you sell. You may sell services, products or both.

Promotion: The act of encouraging acceptance of a product, service or company by mentioning it frequently enough that it is recognized as familiar to the listener; A type of publicity or public relations that creates an impression in the mind of the viewer or listener that is positive and familiar; the process of creating good will in the collective mind of the marketplace; the process of communicating with the public to influence a group to buy your offerings or do business with your company. Promoting is a form of marketing that includes advertising but may include more subtle messages and incentives to buy and may avoid an overt call to action.

Psychographics: The attributes relating to personality, values, attitudes, interests, or lifestyles. A research process that identifies and separates markets into groups based on attitude, interests and opinion clusters (see Value, Attitude and Life Styles).

Sales: The personal or impersonal process whereby the salesperson ascertains, activates, and satisfies the needs of the buyer to the mutual, continuous benefit of both buyer and seller.

Scalable: An adjective that describes applications or systems that are able to grow (scale) to large amounts of users; the ability of a product or network to accommodate growth. Having the ability to increase the number of users, the size of databases and the complexity of the queries and reports without having to modify the structure of the program.

Target market: The group of people you have defined that are most likely to need, or desire your product or service. The people you will target in your promotional campaign.

Unique Selling or Sales Proposition (USP): The quality of a business, product, or service that distinguishes it from everything else in the marketplaces that is similar to it. The required branding element that sets you apart from your direct competitors and gives the buyer a reason to select you as better meeting his or her needs and wants.

Value: This is the worth or price of a product or service; the benefit of a thing in the mind of the buyer; the reason why something is desired.

Vendor: A business that supplies goods or services to other businesses for resale.

WIIFM: An acronym that stands for "What's In It For Me?" this is the predominant question in the prospective buyer's mind and one that should be answered in any advertising or sales script.

ABOUT THE AUTHOR

J ERRY is an Accredited Executive Associate with the Institute for Independent Business. As a result of this accreditation, he established his own company, the **Progressive Business Development Network, LLC** (www.probusdev.net), through which he mentors owners of businesses across the Western Slope of Colorado. He is also a master executive coach who works with C-level executives in transition across the country, helping them to increase their effectiveness as business leaders.

Additionally, Jerry is the President of **Progressive Business Investment Network, LLC,** as a real estate investor with holdings across the country. He is also the President of the **Problem Solution Center, LLC,** through which he provides mediation services across Colorado.

Jerry spent 28 years as an officer in the US Air Force as a bomber pilot and as a personnel specialist, strategic planning expert, and senior training and education expert rising to the rank of lieutenant colonel. During this same period, he founded five successful and profitable private businesses, all of which were subsequently disbanded or sold due to frequent official moves.

After his retirement from the Air Force, Pradier was recruited to reorganize a private security company—the 55th ranked security company in the United States. He subsequently became the company's Chief Information Officer. Continuing his career in the private sector, he has held positions as Corporate Manager and Special Assistant to the CEO before founding his current business enterprise, the **Progressive Business Development Network**. This current endeavor focuses on providing practical management expertise to solve recurring management problems.

Pradier holds masters degrees in Management from Troy State University, European Division, specializing in Marketing and Personnel Management; in Philosophy from the State University of New York at Albany; a certification in Organizational Development from the Air Force's Leadership and Management Development Center; and, a certification in Leadership Development from Harvard University's Kennedy School of Government. He is a published author and speaker on a number of business and personal development topics.

In 2004, he received his accreditation as an Executive Associate from the Institute for Independent Business. In 2005, he became certified as a peer coach to newly accredited Executive Associates. During this same year, he was appointed to Colorado's Small Business Council to serve as a resource to the Governor and the General Assembly on statewide business issues, and serve as a business advocate. In 2007, he was appointed to the Colorado Workforce Investment Board.

Current and past non-profit experience include; Leadership Monterey Peninsula Alumni Association, Secretary and Long-Range Planner; Monterey County Child abuse Prevention Council, Secretary, and Alabama Council on Child Abuse Prevention, Member and Trainer. He is currently on the Glenwood Springs Airport Board and is the finance director on the board of the Glenwood Springs Center for the Arts.

Pradier is a renowned business trainer and presents workshops and seminars for various non-profit and governmental organizations across western Colorado on a wide range of business topics. He trained and certified counselors and instructors for the Northwest Colorado Small Business Development Centers and conducts this training for the ICA in western Colorado. In 2007, he received certification as a mediator through the Institute for Advanced Dispute Resolution of Colorado State University. Pradier also hosts the business development program, *Progressive Business*, broadcast daily on Aspen, Colorado's Grassroots TV.

Jerry may be contacted at jerry@probusdev.net or at www.AskJerry-TheFixer.com for one-on-one advice and guidance.